D1032986

THE
COLOSSUS
OF
NEW YORK

ALSO BY COLSON WHITEHEAD

The Intuitionist

John Henry Days

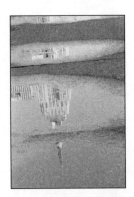

COLSON

WHITEHEAD

DOUBLEDAY

New York

London • Toronto

Sydney • Auckland

THE
COLOSSUS
OF
NEW YORK

A CITY IN THIRTEEN PARTS

PUBLISHED BY DOUBLEDAY
a division of Random House, Inc.

DOUBLEDAY and the portrayal of an anchor with a dolphin are
registered trademarks of Random House, Inc.

Book design by Maria Carella

Photo credits are on page 161.

Library of Congress Cataloging-in-Publication Data
Whitehead, Colson, 1969–
The colossus of New York : a city in thirteen parts /
Colson Whitehead.—1st ed.
p.   cm.
1. New York (N.Y.)—Description and travel.   2. New York
(N.Y.)—Social life and customs.   3. Whitehead, Colson,
1969—Homes and haunts—New York (State)—New York.
I. Title.
F128.55.W54 2003
818'.5403—dc21   2002041691

ISBN 0-385-50794-1

"City Limits" first appeared, in a slightly different form,
in the *New York Times Magazine*.

PRINTED IN THE UNITED STATES OF AMERICA

October 2003
First Edition
1   3   5   7   9   10   8   6   4   2

TO KEVIN YOUNG

CONTENTS

⊰※⊱

THE
COLOSSUS
OF
NEW YORK

CITY
LIMITS

I'M HERE BECAUSE I was born here and thus ruined for anywhere else, but I don't know about you. Maybe you're from here, too, and sooner or later it will come out that we used to live a block away from each other and didn't even know it. Or maybe you moved here a couple years ago for a job. Maybe you came here for school. Maybe you saw the brochure. The city has spent a considerable amount of time and money putting the brochure together, what with all the movies, TV shows and songs— the whole If You Can Make It There business. The city also puts a lot of effort into making your hometown look really drab and tiny, just in case you were wondering why it's such a drag to go back sometimes.

No matter how long you have been here, you are a New Yorker the first time you say, That used to be Munsey's, or That used to be the Tic Toc Lounge. That before the internet café plugged itself in, you got your shoes resoled in the mom-and-pop operation that used to be there. You are a New Yorker when what was there before is more real and solid than what is here now.

You start building your private New York the first time you lay eyes on it. Maybe you were in a cab leaving the airport when the skyline first roused itself into view. All your worldly possessions were in the trunk, and in your hand you held an address on a piece of paper. Look: there's the Empire State Building, over there are the Twin Towers. Somewhere in that fantastic, glorious mess was the address on the piece of paper, your first home here. Maybe your parents dragged you here for a vacation when you were a kid and towed you up and down the gigantic avenues to shop for Christmas gifts. The only skyscrapers visible from your stroller were the legs of adults, but you got to know the ground pretty well and started to wonder why some sidewalks sparkle at certain angles, and others don't. Maybe you came to visit your old buddy, the one who moved here last summer, and there was some mix-up as to where you were supposed to meet. You stepped out of Penn Station into the dizzying hustle of Eighth Avenue and fainted. Freeze it there: that instant is the first brick in your city.

I started building my New York on the uptown No. 1 train. My first city memory is of looking out a subway window as the train erupted from the tunnel on the way to 125th Street and palsied up onto the elevated tracks. It's the early seventies, so everything is filthy. Which means everything is still filthy, because that is my city and I'm sticking to it. I still call it the Pan Am Building, not out of affection, but because that's what it is. For that new transplant from Des Moines, who is starting her first week of work at a Park Avenue South insurance firm, that titan squatting over Grand Central is the Met Life Building, and for her it always will be. She is wrong, of course—when I look up there, I clearly see the gigantic letters spelling out Pan Am, don't I? And of course I am wrong, in the eyes of the old-timers who maintain the myth that there was a time before Pan Am.

History books and public television documentaries are always trying to tell you all sorts of "facts" about New York. That Canal Street used to be a canal. That Bryant Park used to be a reservoir. It's all hokum. I've been to Canal Street, and the only time I ever saw a river flow through it was during the last water-main explosion. Never listen to what people tell you about old New York, because if you didn't witness it, it is not a part of your New York and might as well be Jersey. Except for that bit about the Dutch buying Manhattan for twenty-four bucks—there are and always will be braggarts who "got in at the right time."

There are eight million naked cities in this naked city—they dispute and disagree. The New York City you live in is not my New York City; how could it be? This place multiplies when you're not looking. We move over here, we move over there. Over a lifetime, that adds up to a lot of neighborhoods, the motley construction material of your jerry-built metropolis. Your favorite newsstands, restaurants, movie theaters, subway stations and barbershops are replaced by your next neighborhood's favorites. It gets to be quite a sum. Before you know it, you have your own personal skyline.

Go back to your old haunts in your old neighborhoods and what do you find: they remain and have disappeared. The greasy spoon, the deli, the dry cleaner you scouted out when you first arrived and tried to make those new streets yours: they are gone. But look past the windows of the travel agency that replaced your pizza parlor. Beyond the desks and computers and promo posters for tropical adventures, you can still see Neapolitan slices cooling, the pizza cutter lying next to half a pie, the map of Sicily on the wall. It is all still there, I assure you. The man who just paid for a trip to Jamaica sees none of that, sees his romantic getaway, his family vacation, what this little shop on this little street has granted him. The disappeared pizza parlor is still here because you are here, and when the beauty parlor replaces the travel agency, the gentleman will still have his vacation. And that lady will have her manicure.

You swallow hard when you discover that the old coffee shop is now a chain pharmacy, that the place where you first kissed So-and-so is now a discount electronics retailer, that where you bought this very jacket is now rubble behind a blue plywood fence and a future office building. Damage has been done to your city. You say, It happened overnight. But of course it didn't. Your pizza parlor, his shoeshine stand, her hat store: when they were here, we neglected them. For all you know, the place closed down moments after the last time you walked out the door. (Ten months ago? Six years? Fifteen? You can't remember, can you?) And there have been five stores in that spot before the travel agency. Five different neighborhoods coming and going between then and now, other people's other cities. Or fifteen, twenty-five, a hundred neighborhoods. Thousands of people pass that storefront every day, each one haunting the streets of his or her own New York, not one of them seeing the same thing.

We can never make proper good-byes. It was your last ride in a Checker cab and you had no warning. It was the last time you were going to have Lake Tung Ting shrimp in that kinda shady Chinese restaurant and you had no idea. If you had known, perhaps you would have stepped behind the counter and shaken everyone's hand, pulled out the camera and issued posing instructions. But you had no idea. There are unheralded tipping points, a certain number of times that we will unlock the front door of an apartment. At some point you were closer to the last time than you were to the first time, and you didn't even know it. You didn't know that each time you passed the threshold you were saying good-bye.

I never got a chance to say good-bye to some of my old buildings. Some I lived in, others were part of a skyline I thought would always be there. And they never got a chance to say good-bye to me. I think they would have liked to—I refuse to believe in their indifference. You say you know these streets pretty well? The city knows you better than any living person because it has seen you when you are alone. It saw you steeling yourself for the job interview, slowly walking home after the late date, tripping over nonexistent impediments on the sidewalk. It saw you wince when the single frigid drop fell from the air conditioner twelve stories up and zapped you. It saw the bewilderment on your face as you stepped out of the stolen matinee, incredulous that there was still daylight after such a long movie. It saw you half-running up the street after you got the keys to your first apartment. The city saw all that. Remembers, too.

Consider what all your old apartments would say if they got together to swap stories. They could piece together the starts and finishes of your relationships, complain about your wardrobe and musical tastes, gossip about who you are after midnight. 7J says, So that's what happened to Lucy—I knew it would never work out. You picked up yoga, you put down yoga, you tried various cures. You tried on selves and got rid of them, and this makes your old rooms wistful: why must things change? 3R goes, Saxophone, you say—I knew him when he played guitar. Cherish your old apartments and pause for a moment when you pass them. Pay tribute, for they are the caretakers of your reinventions.

Our streets are calendars containing who we were and who we will be next. We see ourselves in this city every day when we walk down the sidewalk and catch our reflections in store windows, seek ourselves in this city each time we reminisce about what was there fifteen, ten, forty years ago, because all our old places are proof that we were here. One day the city we built will be gone, and when it goes, we go. When the buildings fall, we topple, too.

Maybe we become New Yorkers the day we realize

that New York will go on without us. To put off the inevitable, we try to fix the city in place, remember it as it was, doing to the city what we would never allow to be done to ourselves. The kid on the uptown No. 1 train, the new arrival stepping out of Grand Central, the jerk at the intersection who doesn't know east from west: those people don't exist anymore, ceased to be a couple of apartments ago, and we wouldn't have it any other way. New York City does not hold our former selves against us. Perhaps we can extend the same courtesy.

Our old buildings still stand because we saw them, moved in and out of their long shadows, were lucky enough to know them for a time. They are a part of the city we carry around. It is hard to imagine that something will take their place, but at this very moment the people with the right credentials are considering how to fill the craters. The cement trucks will roll up and spin their bellies, the jackhammers will rattle, and after a while the postcards of the new skyline will be available for purchase. Naturally we will cast a wary eye toward those new kids on the block, but let's be patient and not judge too quickly. We were new here, too, once.

What follows is my city. Making this a guidebook, with handy color-coded maps and minuscule fine print you should read very closely so you won't be surprised. It contains your neighborhoods. Or doesn't. We overlap. Or don't. Maybe you've walked these avenues, maybe it's all Jersey to you. I'm not sure what to say. Except that probably we're neighbors. That we walk past each other every day, and never knew it until now.

THE PORT
AUTHORITY

THEY'RE ALL BROKEN somehow, sagging down the stairs of the bus. Otherwise they would have come here differently. The paparazzi do not wait to take their picture. Barricades do not hold back the faithful. This is the back entrance, after all.

IN THE PARKING berth it is anticlimactic. A man in goggles records the time of arrival. The baggage handler huffs into his palms, one job closer to punching out. Thousands of arrivals every day, they won't stop coming. Different people but all the same. They try to sneak by with different faces but it is no use. They step down the grooved steps, clutching items and the attendant lugs the bags out of the bin, looking for handles. They get excited and jostle: is someone going to steal their bags. They have all heard the stories. One of them has a cousin who came here once and was a victim of street crime. He had to have money wired so he could get home and that was the last time their clan went to New York. There is a thing called three card monte out to get you. They have all heard the stories and they all come anyway. The bags thud on concrete and get taken.

NO MATTER their hometowns, no matter their reasons for sliding cash through ticket windows, on the bus they are all alike. They get on. By the driver they take stock, shoving receipts into pockets and bags. There are some seats in the back. They all want to sit alone. You have never been the first on the bus and had your pick. People have theories about window seats and aisle seats and which areas are safer in the event of a crash. He is unaware that his duffel hits each person on the head as he passes. Is this seat taken, he says, and his measure is taken by his neighbor. Scowls come easy. It only takes five minutes for them to ease into lasting discomfort. If only she could breathe through her mouth for the next thousand miles. She practices a technique. At the next stop people arrange bags and jackets on the empty seats beside them and avoid eye contact or feign sleep when the new pilgrims try to find seats.

—

THERE IS NOT much to occupy them on the highways except intermittent foreshadowings. An industrial park, the confident skyline of a smaller city than the one named on their ripped tickets. Signs on the highway count down miles, sometimes heartening. More furtive things dart from the headlights to escape glimpses. Across three states the empty bottle of juice rolls up and down the bus between shoes and bags. No one claims ownership. Responsible parties pretend not to hear. That is surely a wig two rows up. They try out new positions for their legs. One drawn up and the other wedged into the footrest. Both feet almost in the aisle until the third person trips on them. He has long legs and deserves special rights. The tall man drives his knees into the seat in front of him, squeezing up a chimney. Hers is the only seat that won't recline. The lever has been ripped off and every inclination of her neighbors summons jealousy. Each new combination of limbs might be the one that unlocks the vault of comfort and then sleep. Instead, parts that don't matter fall asleep before their brains. Legs, feet. As they cross state lines, license plates change colors.

SOMETHING HAPPENS TO the bags up there in the baggage racks. When you go to get something out of them they are inexplicably heavier, as if they repacked themselves when you weren't looking. Zippers won't close, hang open in half smiles. Innocuous imperfections in the highway have consequences. The cap of the shampoo loosens itself. Shampoo oozes onto garments, a drop a mile. The smell of shampoo seeps through canvas and reminds whole rows of showers denied them. He falls asleep on the window and when he wakes notices a gray cloud of grease, indentation on a tinted pillow. She thinks she has slept a long time but it has only been ten minutes. Hardly closer.

THANK GOD for the white detachable headrest slipcovers, an invention that saves us from germs. Pat pending. Without gratitude the bus speeds past the factory that manufactures them. The guy in the next seat won't take a hint. She sends signals, glancing at her book, nods or grunts noncommittally but he keeps on yapping. Finally closing the book to submit to prattle. If this loaf of bread lasts for the next three days, he will have nine dollars and seventy-five cents when he gets there. Someone is eating fried chicken, there can be no mistake. The smell of fried chicken makes Rows 8 through 15 hungry and envious until someone cons open a sticky window. The bathroom disinfectant is a genie periodically loosed from its bottle, all out of wishes. Hold it for as long as possible before braving that place. For ten miles of interstate a man inspects his face in the bathroom mirror. Is he actually going to start fresh in a new place with that face of his. If you can endure the verdict of the fluorescent lighting the city will be no problem. He takes a piss and tries not to splash at every latest jolt. Occasionally self-abuse. Through the tiny window left open for ventilation the world blurs. Cool reassurances from moist towelettes. The latch slides to vacant. Then the staggering return down the aisle to find the seat shrunk while you were away.

THE DRIVER IS some kind of priest, changing gears for their salvation. A blank space follows the words, The Name of Your Driver Is. More and more frequently he falls asleep at the wheel for whole seconds. If you ask him to turn the heat up, he might do it. He steers behind dark aviator glasses. He announces a ten-minute rest stop and the prisoners scramble out into the exercise yard. They scramble for fast food, the last chance to eat for who knows how many miles. She recognizes that guy over there from the bus and has a cigarette. As long as he stands there the bus hasn't left yet. Forced to prioritize, some choose food over phone calls to loved ones. Pennies accumulate. It is tense in the fast food lines, how long is ten minutes. To stand there in the parking lot with hot french fries looking at the departing red lights of the bus. Best to cut these missions short. When they get back to the bus there is still plenty of time and they stand there stupidly, too fearful to make another attempt. Everybody has forgotten napkins.

IT IS THE biggest hiding place in the world. The inevitable runaways. The abandoned, only recently reading between the lines. After the beauty contest this is the natural next step. All the big agencies are there. He saved his tips all summer and to see them disappear into a ticket quickened his heart. Not the first in the family to make the attempt. The suitcase is the same one his father used decades before. This time it will be different. The highway twists. She will be witty and stylish there. With any luck he will be at the same address and won't it be quite a shock when he opens the door but after all he said if you're ever in town. Hope and wish. In the light of the bonfire she realized the madness of that place and was packed by morning. They will send back money when they get settled, whatever they can. A percentage. Reliving each good-bye. Practicing the erasure of her accent, she watches her jaw's reflection in the window. Wily vowels escape. No one will know the nickname that makes him mad. This is the right decision, they tell themselves. And then there is you.

THEY REFUEL between towns, gliding down ramps for gasoline. Diesel oases. After all they have been through together, the drivers switch without farewells. What is a passenger to a driver. Apparently those fingerless leather gloves are standard issue. One driver, she never saw his face, just his sure shoulders. The bus changes when you are not looking. It is possible to fall asleep and wake up and everyone is different, all the scalps and haircuts accidentally memorized over miles are transmuted. Everyone reached their destination and got off except for you and it might be the case that all these new people will reach their destinations before you and only you will remain, in this seat, the lone fool sticking for the terminus. In one seat successively sit an infant, a small child, then a teenager and the next occupant will be the next stage older, he is sure of it. But then time is a funny thing on a bus.

—

IF THEY THINK those two words New York will fix them, who are we to say otherwise. They wait for so long to see the famous skyline but wake at the arrival gate and with a final lurch are delivered into dinginess. This first disappointment will help acclimate. The weather is always the same in there. It may be day or night outside, or sunny or rainy outside, but inside the terminal the light is always the same queasy green rays. In effect, no matter what time of day it is, everyone arrives at the same time, in the same weather, and in this way it is possible for all of them to start even. At other gates buses heave in and head out according to schedule. They roar. The fleet returns bit by bit. The buses depart with the ones who need to leave and come back with replacements from every state. The replacements are a bit dazed after the long ride and the tiny brutalities. Row after row they wait to shuffle into the aisle. On her asleep foot she stumbles. He wants to say thanks to the driver but the driver fills out the clipboard and won't look up. In front of the luggage bin they take what is theirs, move bags from hand to hand to discover what is best for the next leg of the trek. Sag on one side. Some take deep breaths. The door opens easily, they are not the first through, and they enter the Port Authority.

MORNING

IN THE MORNING the streets are owned by bread and garbage trucks. Sanitation engineers swashbuckle to sidewalks after scraps, obscure treasure, hoist up chewed-up bread and crusts the bread trucks left days before. Deliver and pick up. Twelve-ton gluttons chew the curb and burp up to windows in mechanical gusts. Where's a rooster when you need one. Instead hydraulics crow. Tabloid haystacks squat. Emptied trash cans skid to anchor corners. Shopkeepers retract metal grates that repel burglars from merchandise unworthy of theft. All this metal grinding, this is the machine of morning reaching out through cogs and gears to claim and wake us. Check the clock to see how much more sleep. Still time. Down there they deliver and pick up. We each have routes we keep to keep this place going.

GODS, HERE'S A TIP. To gain converts, recruit atheists, change your name to Snooze Button. A readily accessible divinity, a reach away, a prayer quick to fingertips if not lips. Like the truest gods it gives them what they already had and wins them through alarm. Exquisite torture of the Snooze Button. Wring a pillow to squeeze out minutes, the stuffing it contains. These life rafts from linen closets. Five more minutes might return you to that dream, the one where you were away and happy. It was good and real and cut off before you got to the best part. Almost there and then beep beep beep. Like the best gods it knows how to parcel out paradise.

UP AND AT 'EM. Pad around and revive. Turn on appliances, lights and coffee machines, radios and television sets. Listen to newscasters: while you were safe in here the world may have lost its way. Let these smoothing voices pat down until you are made. Check the window to discover yourself in a morgue, a white sheet covering your unfortunate acquaintance. So it snowed last night. Take your eyes off this city and it will play tricks. While you are sleeping it pranks to build your character. Where's that trusty sweater. It will keep you warm. Maybe no one will notice it's full of holes.

—

FACE THE DAY well armed with helpful info from morning shows. A tiny incident might shape up into an interesting scandal, cross your fingers. Birthdays of people possessing esoteric secrets vis-à-vis longevity. We could all use a handy computer graphic and earnest newscaster and ominous tagline for this new phase of our lives, yet no technicians scramble to produce it. Check the weather: there's a little cartoon sun over a region you don't inhabit. This is the most important meal of the day: accepting into your gut what lies outside your doorstep. Out of coffee. Out of milk. Out of luck. Late again. Call in sick, or don't. One glimpse into the bathroom mirror proves last night's self-improvement plan to be this morning's abandoned scheme. So nice to wake to your spouse's hip but then remember last night's disagreement and decide you are still angry. Forgetting that when you skip your shower you are paranoid all day.

WEAR YOUR TOTEM item and everything will be okay. If only you'd done laundry, you wouldn't be in this position. Regret, scavenge, assemble. The blessing of a secret stash of matching socks. The name of his cologne is Hamper, Recommended by Four Out of Five Whiffs. She is betrayed. Not once but repeatedly. This morning everything conspires against. Let down by a broken alarm clock, rebuked by work untouched last night, and now this snow. A well-planned assault against equilibrium that will end at midnight, when the spell is broken. Not a single clock offers an encouraging word, not even the one in the microwave, famous for its accelerations. We have been well rehearsed in our responses to first snows and first frosts. We take our places.

PECK GOOD-BYES to loved ones. You don't want to know what goes on in your apartment when you're not around. Before he crosses the threshold he must recite the manifesto that makes him steel. The door clicks locked behind and then outside into cold morning. The wind is a harsh critic, renowned for sardonic turn-of-phrase, but for once it is nice to be free of politeness, to receive the world without sugar coating. That Today Is the First Day of the Rest of Your Life crap. Outside objects are snug in a white coat. Button the top button you save for emergencies, throw fists into pockets. The snow is already shamed and grimed: five minutes is all it takes for this city to break you. Canines add pigment to piles, rescuing snowballs within from mittened hands. As it melts, snow will disinter dog shit, yet no archaeologists rush to catalogue. Fleas of salt scare away snow. Maintenance men shovel snow from walkways to shoo away lawsuits. Along buildings and curbs, herded by shovels and wind, the snow huddles together for warmth. Everybody stick together. We have little else but safety in numbers.

A MOTLEY CREW waits for transportation. Leave the house fifteen minutes later or earlier and join a different cast of characters. This is a whole new troupe with their strange repertoire. Time it right to see your secret crush at the bus stop. Moved away two weeks ago without telling you but keep the fire burning, my faithful. Forget something upstairs and make the calculation. Bitter coalition of the workbound. They hoist the flags of their native countries. Just an hour into her day she sags, already defeated. Frozen eyeglasses fog. Roll past landmarks, we have private landmarks everyone can see. Seeing the particular awning through the bus window that announces he is almost there. Can you make it to the door in time. Pardon me, excuse me, where's the fire. He has timed this route down to the second and today they are whole minutes off and everything is awry.

—

A PATH in the snow. Following in footsteps makes it easy as we retrace each other. No songs or statues for the early pioneers except their footprints. Every uneven step reacquaints you with the hazards of citizenship. So morning becomes required reading, a manual of struggle against odds. The frozen-to-death wait for someone to notice. They walk past him, seeing or not seeing, ignoring or indifferent. Avoid slush and its intimations. Forces work against you to melt your resolve into slush. Put your worst foot forward. As if you were not already wide awake and well shocked. Melting snow drips off awnings. No snow on street grates. Such abominable heat from below, what wouldn't melt. The superstitious and the merely wary avoid walking on the steel doors that speak of the underworld. Gossip tells of people who have fallen into the unseen below. Goblins, hobgoblins, the homeless. Steel rattles under her brave treads and warns. Mornings will kill you with their trapdoors.

SKIRTS ARUFFLE, hats launch, eyes grit up under the effects of this wind tunnel. Things are set fleeing. Hands pat down. Determination sets. This wind will mug you of everything, make you look ridiculous as you try to maintain. It's these tall buildings and their architectural tricks. Shade in summer, cruelty in winter and truth be told it is this season they savor. Bang fingers against thighs to beat warmth into them, give up on ears. Note to self: Get Gloves. Vendors of papers and muffins haunt their staked-out corners. The same greetings to each customer. Remembering how you like your bagel, anointing you a regular with privileges. I like it black. Gooey surprises at the bottom of the coffee cup, dunes of undissolved sugar. His entire shipment of coffee lids is defective, irritating customers one by one. Two drops of java on his shirt is enough to make the day unsalvageable. Pulses quicken, percolating consciousness. Not until the third cup will he be human. Drag knuckles until then.

31

HEADLINES TRY to get under your skin and cheap ink on top of it. Wrassle and grapple newspapers. If only he knew the proper way to fold a newspaper on public transportation. If only my robot double were working, I'd send him to the office in my place. They like him better anyway. Over that stranger's shoulder, a writer of horoscopes is an intimate friend. He looks like an idiot in this suit, but it's the only one he owns and he can mask his too short sleeves by magic-show posture. Too big for these pants and considering that popular weight-loss program. At her bulging waistband the zipper tab stands at attention. Just now noticing the dry cleaner's sabotage and devising ways to hide this treachery through the long day. Little things like that ruin promotions. It popped up on her cheek overnight and now no one will look her in the eye all day. Notice your first wrinkle, it made you late in front of the bathroom sink. No time to buy the advertised creams. First it snows and now this personal frost to consider. Forget what calendars say—it is these unimpeachable signs that tell us when a new season is upon us.

LAST NIGHT hangs heavy in the morning sky, weather that forecasters cannot describe for lack of proper instrumentation. Try to interpret last night's passion. Try to make sense of last night—this time we will make this relationship work despite precedent. The only scholar in the discipline called yourself, never mentored, sans colleagues. Her smell still on him. After work and before sleep you let your true self out for a few hours and now you must pay for it. What were their names and what did it mean. Such is the reach of happy hour and its deceptively long hands. Someone probably deserves an apology. You never made it home. Maybe no one will notice she is wearing the same clothes. No one comments on the strange marks on his neck and when he gets home he will curse each of his coworkers for saying nothing. What will you share around the hypothetical water cooler or that solid coffee station. If you don't plan ahead, who will you be: just another idiot holding a paper cup. Hung over from spirits. How do I smell and is this evil coming out of my pores. Discreetly sniff yourself. All of them have things waiting to come out through their skins. Unmetabolized inadequacy, dread, hope, although no one has told them that this last item has no scent.

SOLDIER ON. Pass the night shift on their way home. They have already seen the new situation on the front but cannot describe, lest you run back to bunker of home. Let us not neglect the children, for they also brave this minefield. They have smaller feet but are not exempt from disaster. Mittens clipped to sleeves. Bent bus passes brandished. Hide a toy in your pocket. He's not supposed to take it to school, but who can dispute the power of cereal box talismans. Instructing kids in the workaday world through elementary threats. If they knew it will always be like this, they would revolt, go back to sleep where they stand, fall to the floor on buses, topple onto sidewalks. The only sane response, really.

PLACES, EVERYONE. Keep this machine up and running. Deliver and pick up. Every day a down payment. Get busy in the fine print of this contract while there is still time. Practice inflections for the big proposal. Devise busywork for the intern. Cram for the big test. After all that fear, the boss won't be in today, the teacher is sick, and instead of what we expected, we have gullible substitutes. This fact summoning from reluctant lips the first smile of the day. All that hustle was for naught you think, but in fact it was down payment. One after the other the long days stretch ahead until the day you decide. Not today. Maybe tomorrow. Take five seconds to collect yourself starting now. Then back to work everybody and I mean it.

CENTRAL
PARK

ON THE FIRST day of spring in search of anti-
dote they seek the park, hardly aware of biological imper-
ative. Everybody has the same idea. After all it's been a
while. They've waited long months for this, have soldiered
through slush and have worn sweaters. So it breaks in them
with a snap, foot on twig: the Park. The one place they forgot to pave over. They'll get around to it someday. Be patient.

SHALL WE GO this way or that. Every day's essential
either-orness made plain made paved in concrete: a forking
path. Debate and deliberation until they sally arbitrarily.
Just minutes in and the afternoon is set in stone. Whole
possibilities canceled by this first mistake. People wear
their first day of spring T-shirts, the true classics of their
ragtag ensembles. Resentment fills the hearts of the regu-
lars. Who are these savages. Every afternoon limping to

this bench with her hoard of crusts. Her reach is audible as pigeons totter forward. Every evening walking the same path to the same tree, just to make sure it is still there. One solid thing in his life. Now these heathens with water bottles and look at that specimen sitting in my favorite spot.

WHERE TO SIT, where to sit. Our whole future depends on this choice. Strangers abound with their customs. A man and a woman pose on opposite benches, taking turns catching each other looking. Such extravagant speculations from so little. So goes the romance of the park bench. No one makes a move. Under the sun minutes expand until she gets up to leave. Wouldn't work out anyway. Shriveled men have determined that the average time spent on a park bench is seventeen minutes. Your tax dollars at work. In their green vehicles the deputies of the Parks Department keep the peace. They know the best spots to get a little shuteye when their bosses go out for lunch. Keep off the grass. This section closed. Scheduled to reopen three weeks ago yesterday. One girl uses chalk to sketch a hopscotch board, another the Virgin Mary. The rain will wash it all away from agnostic cement. Some ducks. He's definitely wearing the wrong shoes. Smile, everybody, smile.

—

WATCH OUT for horses and wake manure. Watch out for humans on conveyances. Trusted servants heave wheel-chaired heiresses. Rollerblading yuppies burn off brunch. Always some jerk on a unicycle. A yogi demonstrates his amazing powers and mimes on their day off expound end-lessly. In the air softballs shuttle, Frisbees wobble and epi-thets hurtle. Some things are more easily caught than others. This gang on skates explodes from the left and right of him and fly from him like sparks. So you lie. Flat on your back on the grass. Such a rich blue. What are you thinking about. Nothing. She calls this rise Heartbreak Hill because that's what it is. For three years out of key with his time he studied the ancient martial arts in order to stand here looking stupid practicing in public. Dead men dyna-mited rock to undo glacial handiwork but holdout boul-ders remain, unwilling to part with the deeds. Climbing across them children find themselves on the moon. This is genuine Manhattan schist. Accept no substitutes. In search of bygone days he wanders. The tree he and his brother used to climb is no longer so tall and kids since have snapped off the branches they made rungs. He climbs up anyway. Thirteen stitches.

—

IT'S A little-known fact that people are buried here but only the murderers know the exact locations. Invisible wet stuff on the ground and here's a dead squirrel. So much for the picnic. Cross-legged summits. Welcome to the Riviera. Mistakes have been made in the area of shorts. This guy's nuts hang out as he sits Indian-style and she should really consider waxing if she's going to leave the house like that. Bushes, hedges, dark thickets. Don't go too far, kids, there are areas used for anonymous sex. Let's have anonymous sex, what do you say. Don't touch it, you'll get rabies. Prod it with a stick instead.

THE FAMOUS photographer prowls here for real-life stuff with his camera as victims enact. Years from now she will see her photograph in a gallery and wonder why she was crying. He touches her arm and says, I just want to make you happy. Oh. Some kids recently fucked in this spot under the eyes of those in the penthouse apartments. Inevitable spike in binocular sales this time of year. The giant digital clock above the corporate headquarters warns them of curfew. He says, See that window, pointing. No, that one. That's where I used to live. The new occupants gloat and glower behind tinted glass. Paperbacks bend on spines. Dogs hike legs. Some of the less talented hippies do a jig.

EMPIRE OF BROKEN teeth, scraped knees and tiny bits of glass. He is the king of the playground thanks to his hormonal problem, stealing toys and cutting line at the slide. His mother pretends not to notice and consults the article in her purse about that new medication. Intrigue by the jungle gym: the twins in striped shirts plan a coup. Parents gossip on benches. See, it runs in the family. Rumor has it this is where she met her new husband; their kids got into a fight in the tree house and they looked into each other's eyes and just knew. Where's her bottle. What's that sound. The swing set squeaks, a gargoyle tuning instruments. Mayo gone translucent in the heat. Under low stone bridges trolls are invisible. He thought this path was the way out but instead it takes him farther in. Then the spectacular malevolence of a cloud. You can see it creeping across the meadow before it hits you. So cold and abrupt. Like a friend.

—

SO MANY PEOPLE running. Is something chasing them. Yes, something different is chasing each of them and gaining slowly. She feels fit and trim. People remove layers one by one the deeper they get into the park. The sweaters keep falling from their waists no matter how they tie them. The matching strides of the jogging pair give no indication that after she tells her secret he will stop and bend and put his palms to his knees. Like some of the trees here, some of today's miseries are evergreen. Others merely deciduous. This is his tenth attempt to join the jogging culture. This latest outfit will do the trick. Pant and heave. How much farther. Reservoir of what. Small devices keep track of ingrown miles. Unfold these laps from their tight circuit to make marathons. It's his best time yet, never to be repeated. If he had known, he would have saved it for after a hard day at the office or a marital argument. Instead all he has is sweat stains to commemorate. One convert says, I'm going to come here every day from now on. It's so refreshing.

WHAT WE REALLY need are popsicles. If they'd foreseen this heat, the vendors would have stocked up on ice. Lukewarm lemonade but who can complain. Let's move to the shade. Fools wade in fountains. Their family looks happier than yours. This is where they came on their first date, so he steers her to this grove and hopes she will realize the error of her ways. She looks at her watch. Sunlight catches on glass surfaces and bits of metal. Glad we came but now I'm tired. It's not really a shortcut, cutting across the park, because there are places he cannot walk, that are fenced off, there are no direct paths and there goes his chance of making the surprise party. Behind that rock they smoke a joint. Next time less spit, please. For an assignment for school he collects leaves and twigs for examination under microscope. Bear away bits and pieces of this place. You probably need a permit.

IT'S GOT BIRDS and a steady ratio of human-to-guano contact. It's got weeping willows. They remind me of me. It has ponds. People can't see themselves and pronounce ponds murky but in fact they are perfect mirrors. Great day to be a caricaturist—everyone remembered to bring their faces. Benign sketches will be forgotten under benches and bus seats. The more damning ones lead to new haircuts. Is my nose really that big. Skin obscured all winter is out of practice. Have I always had this mole and if so is it getting bigger. His conspicuous long sleeves hide hesitation marks, souvenirs of that bad summer. The lines at the fountain are too long. Superpowerful nozzles drench faces. He runs along, shouting encouragement to his kite. Great day for flying a kite. Tried it in the middle of Broadway once, what a disaster. The boy starts spinning around and around in order to get dizzy and look at his funny walk. Pull up your drawers, girl. He says, I wish we had kids, blaming her with his tone. He never comes here even though he only lives two blocks away and now that he has forced himself to take in the sunshine everything is still terrible. Isn't that the cutest puppy. The old philosophers said it best: picking up chicks at the dog run is easy. No particular place to be. Just taking it all in.

GREEN. For whole minutes it is as if you live somewhere else than where you do. And what is that like. Like there are other choices. And then one bullying highrise pokes its head up west, then another, and a whole gang of them east and suddenly come out with your hands up, you're surrounded. Regiments on all sides. Armies don't get better than this. Stray too close to the edge and you'll be reminded as edifices frown down. Not yet. She goes deeper in.

—

THE BENCH she chooses turns out to be the location of the dance performance. Dancers and musicians hang a shingle in a good-luck spot according to their subculture. Just her and them at first but then the drums summon strollers, one couple, then ten, soon swaying human rings. Latecomers want to know what's going on in there. I'm always too late. People can't help themselves and feet tap, fingers tap. After untold basement rehearsals the dancers have it down pat. Look around. Brought together in this moment in a park on the first day of spring. A community. And fancy that in a city. Back to a time before zoning and rebar, one tribe, drums talking. Something that cannot be planned. Everybody knows they must remember this feeling because soon it is back to the usual debasement and they try to remember and then it stops. Cash and coins fill the small basket. Cheapskates avert their eyes and then everybody moves on to that next brief oasis. It never happened. Except her on that bench. She stretches her arms. What a nice day.

ALL AT ONCE they want to go home. Something about the light. Everyone knows how to fold a blanket. Responsible citizens clean up, retrieving bits of themselves from blades of grass. Anything you brought here you must take away. Anything you found here must remain: it can't exist outside. People hear traffic as they get close to traffic and remember rules. Big hungry city but some relief: they know the rules again. At the Don't Walk sign he comes to his senses, possessing dinner plans. He sighs. Glad that's over.

SUBWAY

AFTER THOSE STEPS turnstiles spin and schemes kick in, where to stand and wait. It is hard to escape the suspicion that your train just left, the last squeal of your train drained away the moment you reached the platform, and if you had acted differently everything would be better. You should have left sooner, primped less. Reconsiderations: taking a cab, grabbing a bus, hoofing it. No, it's too far and the train is coming. It must be coming. Why else would you stand there.

THIS IS THE fabled journey underground, folks, and it's going to get a whole lot worse before it gets better. On the opposite track it's a field of greener grass, you gotta beat trains off with a stick. From his secret booth the announcer scares and reassures alternately. The postures on the platform sag or stiffen appropriately. With a dial controlling the amount of static. What are their rooms like, the men at the microphones. One day the fiscal improprieties of the subway announcer's union will be exposed and that will be the end of the hot tubs and lobster, but until then they break out the bubbly. Look down the tunnel one more time and your behavior will describe a psychiatric disorder. It's infectious. They take turns looking down into darkness and the platform is a clock: the more people standing dumb, the more time has passed since the last train. The people fall from above into hourglass dunes. Collect like seconds.

THERE'S A CULTURE for platforms and a culture for between stations. On the platform there are strategies of where seats will appear when the doors open, of where you want to be when you get off, of how to outmaneuver these impromptu nemeses. So many variables, everyone's a mathematician with an advanced degree. Wait. Those elephantine ears of hers. Does she know something he doesn't, she's moving closer to the edge, and then he hears the roar, too. The herd trembles, the lion approaches, instincts awaken. The jaws slide apart and the people step inside. Various sounds of gorging.

—

WHICH CAR will you choose. Take your pick. In the happy-go-lucky car the wattage of their smiles brightens the tunnels. In the no-particular-place-to-go car they are recumbent. In the going-to-be-late car the grimace festival is in full swing. In the had-a-long-day car there are no seats. So again we must ask, which car will you choose. Dilemmas escalate. Can I make it to the seat before she gets there. Their eyes meet and they calculate distance. Stared down once again he gives up, such is his lot, and he leans against the conductor's door. At the next station the conductor has to shove against to get out.

LET 'EM OUT, let 'em out. From stop to stop oblong advertisements suddenly get interesting in a strange sort of way. Along the fungi hall of fame we are introduced to ailments. Has anybody ever in history copied down the phone number of the dermatologist with the sinister name. After all these years he still hopes the needy will receive his revolutionary technique but for now must make do with these flimsy cardboard advertisements. You are inducted. Advertisements that meant nothing to you last week are now your last hope. Look above their scalps. That is salvation up there and maybe a poem.

—

ONLY AFTER a while does he notice her and give up his seat to the elderly lady. The pregnant lady, the man with the leg injury. His unfortunate good manners. Scootch over. Scootch away from the smelly wino. It's just a piece of candy wrapper but no one touches it for fear that it contains the world and so one empty seat on the crowded subway car. Spying an empty seat but when you get there soda sloshes. At the next stop someone sits in it and he feels bad for not warning him but that's not his job really. Realization drains into the man's face as the soda leaks through: now there are two seats wet. A vehicular library. Bibles and bestsellers keep away the other citizens' faces. Newspapers in foreign languages cater to communities. Accidentally touch the underside of the seat and become an advocate for stricter gum laws. Halfway to the interview she notices two typos in her résumé. The man on her right snoozes amid the jolts and leans his head on her shoulder as if he sensed her angelhood. Too polite, she resorts to ineffectual nudges. It's kind of funny, actually. The woman across the car smiles at her plight. At the next station he awakes mysteriously and bolts.

—

D O N O T hold the doors, do not lean against the doors, the doors are not your friend. If you want friends start a club based on mutual interests, do not come into the subway. He is perfectly attired save for his socks, which mark and doom him when he crosses his legs. The homeless man hopes the next car will be more generous. The musician with the broken trumpet irritates. People examine the scuff marks on their shoes when he walks by with his cup. You reach into your pocket for change but forgot you used it on that phone call and isn't it awkward with that guy sticking his hand out. Folding his coat on his lap to hide the sudden inexplicable erection.

O U T O F the tunnel and suddenly elevated. Second-floor city. Looking into apartments, browsing lives and what people throw up on their walls. There are never any people in the apartments. Scores of tenement tableaux registering on the eye mostly as moods, mostly sad and blue. He can see through the windows into the next car and wonders if they are happy in there. Cars start off at the same station and then diverge. Two different lines with estranged termini, kin despite complicated parentage. And they're off. His car takes an early lead, a window length, and then through struts the competition surges ahead. His car catches up. They meet eyes. Their expressions do not change. This place has practiced them in stuffing down weakness. And then that other car begins its submarine dive here, the tracks go deeper into the earth on their own secret route, west or north, no time for farewells. Let's call it a draw. There's always next time.

A PERCENTAGE about to get off stands too soon. About to get off but jumped the gun and it's all black out there. Vaguely embarrassed. Their seats are already filled. Should he switch here, he wonders, as the cars pull in to existential station. Run. They all dash out to the local, some come the other way to the express, in rare cases transfers end up taking each other's seats on the other train. It happens less frequently with these modern cars, on these modern tracks, but sometimes the lights go out and what do you do then with all these monsters beside you. I remember when this used to cost a dime. If this car were suddenly transported to a desert island and they were like stuck there she could maybe make out with that guy. Why are you standing so close to me. Is he trying to read the map behind her or interviewing her scalp: you make the call. Here it is, the class trip in their identical day camp T-shirts. Peppy adults herd and hector. Everybody stick together. Pick a buddy. Have you once again picked the car with class trip. Stuck here with these midget mewling things. Too young for sex they punch each other in the arm.

WE ARE STUCK in the tunnel on account of a police action at the station ahead of us. We are stuck in the tunnel on account of a sick passenger on the train in front of us. Him again, that rheumy bitch. For someone so sick, he sure gets around a lot. Perhaps he is merely more evolved and now allergic to filth and speed. Take up a collection to subsidize a private limo for the sick passenger. The announcer tries to give information. Every mishap down here radiates outside this car, generating excuses arguments likely stories. What happens down here fertilizes that up-top world. There are slim walkways for mole employees to walk on without being crushed. They have day-glo vests and a deep longing for those who rush by. They get paid to be subterranean. To know what it is to work down there. She finds grit in her fingernails as she speeds past them.

STRAPHANGING actually an antiquated term. It's all metal now, swiveling commas, poles in perpendicular arrangements. But they still hang, still droop, dangle on curled fingers. Feet next to feet. The pole is sickeningly warm God forbid moist from previous fingers. Microbes rejoice. His hand slides slowly down the pole, touching her fingers, so she bids her fingers retreat. He chases, they bump again, she retreats farther. Their hands slide down, all without eye contact. One of many daily contests here. Beware of frottage. Readjust your balance at every lurch. If you don't know what time it is, wait for a peek when he changes his grip. Even if they pulled into his station right now it would be too late.

HIS HEART speeds up before his mind can process the fear: haven't they been between stations for too long. Stationless for quite a while now and it is quite disconcerting. Suddenly realizing you've taken the express. Past familiar stations, farther than you have ever gone before. Neighborhoods you have heard of but never reckoned. Burrowing under a river, good God the horror of a whole different borough. It could be apocalypse above for all you know and who wouldn't think disaster, stuck in the tunnel like that. Isn't this slope just a little too deep. Going down. They have laid rail into the center of the earth and this is where we are going. There are tales of phantom lines, haunted stations. We've all sped past ghost stations where the exits have been bricked up and graffiti warns in looping letters. Abandon all hope. There is no escape if the train stops at ghost stations and we will mill in purgatory. That explains it: he died today without knowing and now this train is taking him to the underworld. Then you suddenly pull in and have to pay again to switch.

THEY ROCK in unison, at least they agree on that one small thing. Check their wallets—the denominations won't jibe. Review their prayers—the names of their gods won't match. What they cherish and hold dear, their ideals and shopping lists, are as different and numerous as their destinations. But all is not lost. Look around, they're doing a little dance now in the subway car and without rehearsal they all rock together. Shudder and lurch together to the car's orchestrations. Some of them even humming. Everybody's in this together until the next stop, when some of them will get off and some others get on. This is your stop. Get off. Get off now and hurry, before you are trapped in the underworld.

RAIN

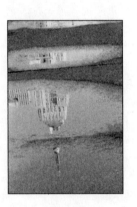

O U T   O N the street they hardly notice the clouds
before it starts raining. The rain comes down in sheets.
Drenched all at once, not drop by drop. The first drop is
the pistol at the start of the race and at that crack people
move for shelter, any ragtag thing, they huddle under
ripped awnings, the doorway of the diner, suddenly an ap-
petite for coffee. Pressed up against buildings as if on the
lam. Little sprints and dashes between horizontal cover.
Dry here. Surely it will stop soon, they think. They can
wait it out. It cannot last forever.

S U S P E C T I N G such an eventuality, the umbrella
salesmen emerge to make deals. They wait all week for this
and have ample supply of one-dollar bills. The virtues of
their merchandise are self-evident. She carries an umbrella
every day no matter what the news says because you can
never tell and is vindicated by moisture. It pops open. The

doused press down on reluctant buttons and the mechanisms pop open. Underneath their personal domes, they are separated from the peasants. To be this easily isolated from all worry. The silver tips dart and jab for eye sockets. Probability says many are blinded by pointy umbrella spokes and you are surely the next victim. At the corner he wrestles with a ghost for the soul of his umbrella. The gust gains the upper hand as he waits for the light to change and the umbrella is ripped inverse. Many are lost. The wounded, the fallen in this struggle, poke out of trash cans, abandoned, black fabric rippling against split chrome ribs. This is their lot. Either in the trash can or forgotten in the restaurant, the movie theater, the friend's foyer, spreading their slow puddles across floors. Forming an attachment to an umbrella is the shortest route to heartbreak in this town. Any true accounting would reveal that there are only twenty umbrellas in this city, in constant movement from palm to palm. Bunch of Lotharios. So do we learn loss from umbrellas.

THE NEW RIVERS along curbs shove newspaper and grit to gutters. Too big to squeeze through grates the garbage bobs in place like the unstylish waiting for nightclub doors to open. The liquid sinks below. The alligators don't mind. Eventually a clog sends a puddle advancing. A sliver of moon, the surface of the puddle is tormented by brief craters. Each drop explodes and extends the surface of the puddle. Doing their part for the water cycle, the bus wheels return the puddle to air again. Complacent beneath her umbrella she is thoroughly soaked when she stands too close to the curb. The enemy came from below. The metropolitan transit authority reinforces old lessons: every puddle wants to hug you. If not heavy motor vehicles then it is the children in their bright red boots detonating puddles on people. Knock it off.

IT FINDS the nape of your neck easily. It traces the length of your spine greedily. The long list of errands shrinks into what people can do in the least amount of water. So much for the dry cleaning. All over town the available number of cabs shrinks as thin fingers tilt and quiver at the edges of traffic. The bastard one block upriver gets it before you can stick a hand out, just as you are someone else's bastard one block downriver. Epithets are tossed against the flow of traffic, upon the unbeknownst. Everybody just wants to get home, so they make calculations and jockey. What's a better block for a cab. East or west, up a street or down. Schemes multiply and divide the longer you stand there. The supercomputer of cab-catching. Sixth Avenue is uptown and Seventh is down, important variables. The time of day, the direction and force of the wind, sun spots, that Pacific typhoon, all important considerations in the acquisition of a cab. She hailed it because she thought it was empty, but it speeds by with smug fares in the backseat who do not even notice her. Day like this all it takes is a little cab fare in your pocket to become royalty.

COUPLES FORCED into doorways kiss, coached by the cinema. One of them says one two three and they make a break out of the latest slim refuge. They are reminded after a few steps of how cold the rain is. They stop at the next outpost to catch their breath and forget how cold the rain is. This is the start of her long illness. The wrapping would be ruined by the water so he holds the present under his coat, lending to his belly the contours of an absurd pregnancy. She hides in the bus stand. She hasn't taken the bus in years and feels a secret terror. Pressed up against other people: what's the point of money. In shelter they make plans. He doesn't know where he is supposed to be because the paper got wet and now the address is a smudge. Lost at intersections. Look at all the trenchcoats—it is the detectives' convention come at last to take care of all our loose ends. Up in all the windows, leaning on the sills, the dry people look down on the street and think, Glad I'm not out in that. As if they are without problems. Open half an inch, the window in the next room is still open wide enough to get the floor wet before they notice.

65

A MAN of liberal convictions, he got this umbrella by pledging money to public radio. It sends the message that he supports public radio. Has a matching tote bag. Now no one will suspect she has been crying. After a block it is evident that they both will not fit under the compact umbrella and one must make do with a dry shoulder. Is this the end of their love. The weekend outdoorsman strides through in his appropriate gear, this is no cliff face or ravine, and he is well equipped. Her glasses are too wet to see through so she takes them off and squints through precipitation. When she gets inside she'll use up napkins. Unable to decide which side of the bed is more comfortable, the windshield wipers toss and turn. Sleepless like rivers. How swiftly the newspaper becomes a sodden brick over his head. It doesn't keep him dry at all despite clichés. From street level as he looks up into the clouds each advancing drop is elongated, a comet, until it hits his cheek and crashes. On his lips it doesn't taste so bad. One drop hits his eye and stings more than mere water should. He blinks. Sooty streaks trail under windowsills. Every building a coquette, a face powdered by industry. This so-called cleansing leaves behind more than it washes away. But then few things are as advertised.

NEW SOCKS tint soaked toes blue. The shoes take forever to dry. Last time it rained he put them under the radiator and hours later they were warped and twisted, as if it were agony to let the water go. Next time he will remember the water repellent spray. It is available at local pharmacies. Secure in her foresight, she wonders about the etymology of the word galoshes. Of course it is a ridiculous thing to walk around with plastic bags tied over your shoes, but do you know how much these things cost. The puddle at the curb is deeper than it looks, an ancient loch. Trying to jump over it you fall short and the lagoon spills into your shoes. Tonight the bunched balls of his socks will dry and stiffen into dingy fists, and roll under the bureau, where they will hide for months and foment.

—

HE CLIMBS UP the steps and realizes that while he was in the subway the whole world changed. It's all gray. Pull lapels tight. Only the gargoyles seem happy, up there on the roofs. If you're lucky when you die, you become one and get to hang out here forever. He says, You think the money they get paid, the weathermen would get it right for a change. Remembering only disasters. The stock boy rips up cardboard boxes to lay down in the entrance of the store. All our vain gestures. It makes the boss happy, it's how they did it in the old days. The newspaper vendor takes all these wet bills in stride. But no one wants to buy a wet newspaper. The stacks got wet before he could cover them up. In the competing store across the street the news piles up underneath a transparent tarp. Survival of the fittest, but of course he is not saddled with an idiot nephew. In the phone booth preparing for the next sortie. Lay all that money out for the hairdresser and now this. They will drag their feet across doormats and track floors nonetheless. Identical twins wear identical yellow slickers, out of which identical noses poke. What's this in the rain-coat pocket. Apparently the last time it rained he saw a ro-mantic comedy.

—

AT THE CORNER it's worse, thrown into their faces like needles or proof. The wind whips it around. Once they find a parking space they decide to wait it out and make out, tilting the car seats back to uncomfortable angles. A nipple gives against a thumb. Once the engine is off they can make out the rain's true incantation on the roof of the car and clench each other tighter. Safe here. The talk always comes around to the weather. Underneath the scaffolding the conversations among strangers range from grunts to bona fide connections. Quite serendipitous. It leaks. From block to block the people display an assortment of strides, every station between a walk and a run. Each has a personal strategy of how best to move in this. The best of them gave up long ago. The best of them cease stooping, stand up straight, stop dodging, take it as it comes. Apparently they are supposed to get wet, so they give in. It is like letting go of something and a small miracle wrung from accident. Walking slowly and naturally in this downpour, they are avoided by the more sensible, who walk swiftly around them, unsettled by these strange creatures. Citizens of a better city.

—

IT STOPS. From the river you can see the clouds haunch over adjacent boroughs. What transpired is a problem for sewers now, out of sight and out of mind. Snapping the umbrella open and closed as if it will scare the water off. It pulsates like a jellyfish in bleak fathoms. She tries to button the strap on her umbrella but keeps losing the snap in the folds. Now her hands are all wet. Some people think it's a trick and keep their umbrellas open for blocks just in case. They walk out of the movie theater and say to each other, Did it rain, pointing at puddles. Yes, they are sure of it, something happened and they missed it.

BROADWAY

ONCE A YEAR he takes the walk. There can be no destination. No map. Live here long enough and you have a compass. Who among them can complain, unanimous weather sparks the same phrases downtown and up: Nice out, isn't it. Borough to borough. So he walks. He will ask no questions this day. The street will not scheme this day. Let it happen. These are the terms of the truce he has made with Broadway.

WALK. Hands in pockets or hands rowing through this surf. It will not matter. No outsmarting. Only suckers try to double-cross Broadway and it always ends up in one-way tickets out of town. Atop poles, street signs name distance. The names of men of substance haunt street signs until they are exorcised by numbers. When they run out of names intersections opt for mathematics, but what kind of equations emerge from such uneven terms, Broadway times Eleventh Street equals what. Must have left my abacus in my other pants. Signs go, Last Chance and Everything Must Go. For a limited time only you can have my heart on layaway. Around him they all have payment plans, arrangements to pay for what they want. And what is he after. He walks.

N I C E   O U T , isn't it. Children avoid fissures in the sidewalk for fear it will give their mothers a spinal injury. Like a child walking in a straight line no matter who what gets in the way. A vow against swerves. See how long you can do it. Obstacles obstruct, the ones on the street and the ones he carries with him. Look down at all that stuff in the cracks in the sidewalk. Let us organize a salute to all the plucky weeds in this town, all those anonymous flowering strivers, with their intrepid shoots and improbable points of purchase. Such exemplary citizens. Seeds seek grime, no shortage of grime, no lack of cracks for grime. This place is falling apart, after all. If you listen close you can hear it. Day by day you contribute to it. You think this place sucks the life from you but in fact it is the opposite. This bosom.

—

WALK AND FALTER in its great rut. It bulldozed across the city, grinding through grid. Diagonal across appalled avenues, scaring parks out of the way, squeezing buildings into flat iron. At night a well-lit scar. In the daylight Everest. All of you, walk. We grunt and moan. As if this road were not more or less level but jungle path. Just hours before, rush hour made a trail. Trampling, taming inclines, making mistakes for them. But the undergrowth has burst up to flail eyes since, shrubbed up to fill footprints, and now all of them are scouts bending back mean branches. Natives and tourists alike bat at assorted mosquitoes. He's lived here all his life. Sometimes he leaves but he's never been good with languages and two feet over the state line is a foreign tongue. Tourists discover what he takes for granted. They torture guidebooks and argue, say, We've passed this way before, traveling in circles like the best old-timers. In this city you always end up where you began. Settle for extending the radius bit by bit, give up on more. He's lived here all his life and friends flee and she fled, too, but Broadway is still here. He walks and pushes against. Keep pushing and you just might increase your radius. Savor hard-won inches.

TRAPPED AT CORNERS, waiting for the light. They catch up to him. Why bother to overtake if they're all conniving tortoises, ratified by fable. Hey, here comes the league of sexy moms. Pushing carriages, tilting at curbs, steering progeny across pavement. To be safe and unknowing again. Tiny fingers grab air above cribs. People try to make other people's babies smile as they wait for the light to change. Strangers are always blurry. A brigade of pregnant ladies waddles with dignity. Three months from now they will blossom into sexy moms, but for now they seek the store that sells clothes for unborn citizens. Uniform them quickly in black. Fetuses fret about what zip code they'll end up in, tapping against membrane in morse code: renting is for suckers. Too young to know that the womb schools the dimensions of a studio apartment. Contemplate dimensions, this citified dementia. The sky has so much square feet when you're allowed to see it between buildings. All together now: we've been ripped off. But breaking the lease at this point is impossible.

THE LIGHT CHANGES and he has that wish again: that every step he ever took left a neon footprint. Every step, from his first to these. That way he could catch up with himself, track himself through city and years. See that the last time he walked this block he was tipsy or in love. Here determined, there aimless like today, no particular place to go. If he could see his footprints, he'd know his uncharted territories, what was yet, and where never to return. Some of the old stores are gone since last time. What comes at their addresses is bright and shiny like new keys. New keys fit new locks. It is rare here that the new establishment is more downscale and if only he could make his self and ideas like real estate: ever higher. God knows he has tried to keep up with the changing market but his new shirt will only go so far—once they step inside they recognize the same old merchandise and demur. He has swept up, his brain gets so dingy sometimes, but they will not see his renovations and he is a dead trade, something remembered only by old phone books. Blacksmith, knife-sharpener. Walk faster.

WALK UNTIL you drop. Past places he has only been in once and never again, a pizza shop, a greasy spoon, that were refuge on a night or an afternoon, because he didn't want to be early, because he was between appointments, because he had been hit by the big fear. For ten minutes or half an hour he loitered over the counter, ignored by waitresses or nibbling baked goods, once and never again and now the place is monument to that day, for years and years, windows a little grimier, signs a little more faded until one day it will be a pet store. Walk past that refurbished window without thought, forget you ever stopped there once, new ownership proving relocation of those old yous. Believe this, evicting the truth of things.

AT TIMES like this recalling a few verses from the latest self-help book may be beneficial. To live so close to Broadway, in its radiation day after day. It will make you sick. On this stretch doormen keep out the diseased riffraff, sorting them from the more luxurious epidemics upstairs. On that stretch the dishes never get done until all three plates are dirty, freeing tenants to scribble fraudulent postcards to places they never should have left. And who lives on your floors, your assorted transients and shut-ins. Such a strange bunch. Such thin walls in this place. Ire and compassion have been neighbors for years, eavesdropping on arguments and clucking tongues, but they haven't seen each other for years. Some of them don't last. Optimism skipped out on the rent a while back, but the cynic in the penthouse won't leave until led out by marshals. They lug their suitcases up the ave, on the move once again. There are always cheaper residences if you're willing to give up your principles. Sign here. Give deposit. They will credit-check your soul.

WALK UNTIL your heart grows heavy with freight. He has fraught corners—some places he passes give him the creeps. Their first date in this restaurant, their last date in that restaurant. His ex used to live upstairs. They made out on that stoop and passersby heckled his technique. He had to make that call, it was very important, and the public phones on this street were cursed, did not work, devoured quarters, and it was disastrous. He has fraught corners and you have yours. Avoid them because you don't want to be reminded. Pavement that remembers a night best forgotten. Potholes that remind you of sunken places in your spirit. See it this day and proclaim, This block's got nothing on me. To be free of all that came before, to mold your face to the cliché of this place. Pick your self. Be famous and celebrated. Be a modern artist: pick a busy intersection and proclaim it your masterpiece. The critics love it, applaud your sense of color, wonder how you got the faces like that. An undercurrent of metropolitan alienation, says one. Like the best art, it was right in front of you all along but now you see it for the first time. Like the best art, it will outlast you.

—

EVERYBODY remembers the city. Some people the city remembers. He is disappearing with every step. Who is he among that crowd. Pick him out among the great unwashed. Wouldn't it be funny if the city actually gave a damn about you. If you made your mark despite odds, if all this step-taking was actually alms-giving and in one unlikely moment after all these years this place smiled upon you. It would happen like this, on an afternoon much like this, when you are between corners and it begins. Every building is somehow a place you have lived in, good times peer out from between curtains. All the streetlights have agreed to grant you speedy passage, safe passage. That would be something. He trips. His shoes are untied. This is Broadway after all and it will undo you bit by bit.

WALK FARTHER. These things float up and what's a boy to do. Have these mannequins no shame. What are they wearing, what's up with their nipples and can I get a date. If only there were zoning laws to regulate strange thoughts. Keep them in other neighborhoods. Only after a few blocks is the sadism of the shoe designer evident. Shop in stores for things, shop on streets for people. You know what you want on your skin. What you choose will wear on you. Forget this block because there's nothing in your size. There's always another across the curb and maybe it will be better. Cross quickly and cross fingers, too, tell yourself, Maybe the next block will be better.

THIS IS WHERE they shot that scene from that movie, you know, the one about that guy. The whole city is make-believe after all. Not famous, merely famous-looking, but he really works it. The real celebrities leave craned necks in their wake. I didn't know he was so short. The uncensored director's cut of his present state of mind would include multiple shootings, not one bludgeoning and untold car crashes. But he doesn't have the budget and has to make do with cheap special effects, manic horn-honkers, and obscene gestures. One take unrehearsed may-hem, roll camera, roll sound. Around him people make their musicals, inducting extras from those around them, casting bit players in their big-budget technicolor extrava-ganzas. No duets, please, no one else to grandstand in the spotlight. The other pedestrains hit their marks, fall dead, and he's the last man alive in a lonely city finally drama-tized. Dance over prostrate bodies as music swells. Every car passing blares this season's inescapable hit. That radio station and its payola choices. One car passes and another car or storefront picks up the baton to make sure the lyrics are always on your lips. What's the name of this song, anyway.

WALK TO DRIVE the point home with your feet as if making wine. From gutters, rats exclaim in gutter chorus; life is an argument with the world over time. If anyone were listening, it'd be worth the breath. People on cell phones realize they were cut off blocks ago and wonder if they have the courage to repeat their words. Mixed messages, lost signals. The masters of billboards shuffle messages and enticements, hector and hang above street level. Airbrushed anatomical parts. He receives word of a remarkable new treatment or other indispensable thing. Lacking a pen he tries to memorize the phone number, repeating it to himself in a singsong way until more vulgar ditties shoulder it aside, bassoon of buses rumbling to beat the light, high-heel castanets on cement, and soon all he has is two digits left and his own lost cause. If he had the money he would advertise his weakness on every billboard, along the brick walls of prewar buildings, and hire the squirrelly and deranged to hand out leaflets on busy corners: This is me. But no one would buy the merchandise because they scour billboards for what they don't have and I got enough mirrors at home. Buy anything in this city and it just adds up to empty plastic bags. Empty plastic bags accumulate in soft white mountains. Where is the vigilante or rogue cop who will rid our streets of these empty plastic bags. Husk of need. Crumple them into each other to save space. Mash down all your unruly things. Make them into wine.

YOU NEED giant's legs to make progress but it is indisputable: he is walking faster. Without knowing it, he found a way into the street's rhythm and isn't it a catchy beat, making his feet sledgehammers, into percussive remaking. Step aside, you urban galoots, move along, you shuffling denizens. He's coming through, hitting his stride. Don't Walk switches to Walk the second he hits the curb. The biggest delivery trucks simper and stall, break route. Shopkeepers close shop early for a glimpse, crowd the curb waving his flag, this is something to tell grandchildren. No dog has soiled his path, he does not waver and now the orchestra begins in earnest, he will have his musical after all, nimbly moving in their tuxedos and ball gowns they dive in, rehearsals tuned to this moment. This is my city. He's the King of Broadway, summoning anthem from potholes and sewer grates. The infrastructure is weak and aged and solid only in one place—under his feet. It will lift him up. There's an armor the city makes you wear and look at him defenseless, breastplate and helmet dropped back blocks ago, no arm among enemies strong enough to string the arrow that could pierce his skin. Rendering all cowards. Let us bow. No one bows. This kingdom is interior.

H E W A L K S and then he slows. Kinda tired. No small bit hungry. Scrutinize menus in windows for hearty fare. The prices are outrageous, he checks his wallet and touching his pocket becomes mortal again, reduced to what he pays in rent. No more strolling, he must stop, because Broadway only gives this once a year, and grudgingly. It's the little taste that makes them go, and keeps them here year after year for these key afternoons. It gives this. Broadway is generous and knows that if it did not dollop out, it would be dried up. These occasional gifts cost nothing. Terrible and generous. Broadway knows that every footfall is its heart beating, that we keep its heart beating, that it needs suckers and citizens to keep its blood flowing. Broadway knows that if this secret ever got out it would be empty, so periodically it offers a glimpse. It costs nothing, this harmless jousting.

H E ' L L   B E   B A C K next year. Around the same spot on the calendar depending on frontal systems and his own inner weather. Because they understand each other, him and Broadway. He will come once a year until he dies and another takes his place. Move those feet. Walk and walk. These are the terms of the truce he has made with Broadway.

CONEY
ISLAND

SUCH A MULTITUDE of stenches means it must be summer. It's the baking asphalt that adds that special piquancy. Discomfort without end, surely this planet is hurtling into the sun. Some cavort like idiots in uncapped hydrants, others head for the edge of town. South, to the beach where a broom of briny air sweeps away this miserable funk. So they fall to the bottom of the subway map, settling there like loose change in various denominations. What they will find under their feet will not be pavement but something shiftier.

ALL TOMORROW'S sunburns gather in wait. Heads dart to and fro as they seek the right spot. Homestead and land grab. This must be the place. Try to remember your personal formula for comfort on a beach, the whole towel thing. Sizzle on the griddle. How to serve man. Gritty evidence of the last visit to the beach clings to the neck of the bottle of suntan lotion. In unison ask, Can you do my back. The sun sets this melting pot to furious boil, brings it all to the surface, the ancient liaisons, the hidden complexions. That extra seasoning. The struggles of everyone's ancient tribes are reduced to how their descendants fare against ultraviolet. People emphasize particular ideas they have about their bodies via too-tight tops, trunks, and T-shirts. Take it all off and don't forget your favorite scars.

EVERYTHING disappears into sand. Objects get lost in sand the way people get lost in streets. There is refuge on the shores of the new world. This is the cozy retirement community for pull-up tabs that have not been manufactured in years, cigarette butts that have seen better days, limbs of crabs. Wood drifts over from native lands. Naturalized styrofoam bits recite pledges and names of presidents at the slightest provocation. Dirty gulls patrol beats, sidestep seaweed bums and their sob stories. Rumor has it someone over there is eating a sandwich. Scavengers peck away, undertake vain missions. Flies buzz and hop over the dead and the dead-seeming. The crazy guy with the metal detector zigs and zags in efficient search pattern or out of habit to avoid teenagers' thrown projectiles. His take-home pay is quite astounding. The number of house keys lost this day will fall within the daily average of lost house keys. Hypocrites complain about the quality of the sand, as if they are not blemishes on its expanse, and scavengers, too, ripping little shreds of comfort from an afternoon.

FRONT LINE in the ancient blood feud between city and nature. What side are you on. Every grain a commando on recon probing for weakness and reporting back. Here are some places sand gets into: eyes, sandwiches, shoes, under beds, scalps, carpets, car floors. Crotches and brainstems and decision-making places. Kids with pails move this bunch of sand from here to there to undo the secret design of tides. Aeons in the making and now it's all ruined. Rule is, violence on purpose and beauty by accident. Their castles rise proudly from soggy plots of real estate, yet despite their enthusiasm a very small percentage of these children actually go on to careers in construction, it's very strange. School's out for the summer but sand is an elementary with lessons. What they shape are cities, no less so for being soft and miniature. Imposition of human order on nature. Sand slips through fingers but no one takes the hint. Our juvenile exercises. What they build cannot last. Fragile skylines are too easily destroyed.

THIS STRIP piggybacks one of the world's magic meridians: keep swimming and you'll end up in England, keep digging and you'll end up in China. So they say. Children yo-yo at the tideline, run in when it seems safe and out when a wave approaches. Depressing mechanical regularity. Mimicking parents and ruthless commute. Sometimes a workweek will grind you into sand, pulverize you into particles. Those who live near expressways recognize the sound of waves. The ocean traffics in ebb and flow, that's its business. Parents surge to teach offspring how to swim. Close your eyes. That wasn't so bad now, was it, says mother to child. He spits out seawater. Riptide and undertow are the world's hands grabbing to save you from cities and their influence. The unseen infrastructure of waves. Events a thousand miles away find their final meaning in these gentle little consequences begging at the shore. Do the dead man's float and drop out of society, no sound, no weight, just you and the forces that pushed you here, set you apart. Anchorless. So safe. Is it possible to stay here, renounce the city, swim the other way. The direction of their final strokes this day is an oath of fealty. Look at this pretty shell.

E V E N   O U T   H E R E still too close to neighbors. Horizontal tenement. Loathe neighbors and their loud boorish talk and unfortunate ditties. Envy neighbors on their well-equipped expedition. Yeah, they know how to do it right, with their everlasting cooler and state-of-the-art collapsible seating. What will they pull out next, a Grillmaster 9000 or merely a famous chef. Just when you get settled a breeze or hooligan ruins things. The insult that made a man out of Mack. Please adjust: parts squeezing out of bathing suits, parts having natural reactions to changing temperatures, the bashful edges of the towel, your attitude because it's really getting on my nerves I go to all this trouble why can't you just enjoy yourself for once. Probably not the right time for a sexual reverie but the view argues otherwise. All that stuff they hide when they dress up in civilization. Don't blink or else you'll miss it—that father's annual display of affection toward his son. Seeing this is like looking at the sun. It can blind you.

—

OUT THERE slow barges cart away tires and exiles, black arrowheads sailing through blue air. Wooden contraptions provide sure footing. Along the top of the pier, fishermen skewer hope on hooks and drop this bait, wait for a little nibble. Along the sides of the pier, barnacles cling with telltale rent control tenacity. Up and down the boardwalk visitors establish their cruising speed. Underneath the boardwalk is where they store failed mayoral candidates. Improbable clam shacks. Hot dog vendor to the world. What was true for citizens a hundred years ago remains so. Generation after generation marvel over the salt air as if they are the first to remark upon it. They keep to themselves the odd feelings brought on by the novelty of a horizon after so many horizonless days. What to do with these notions. Old-timers have seen it all before. We're the reruns they can't help watching. Old-timers will tell ya that every plank on the boardwalk has a story to tell and a secret name. This is in fact untrue. It's just dead wood after all.

OFF SEASON this place is dead. Don't tell anyone but the Wonder Wheel is a gear in the great engine of the metropolis and when it stops moving systems fail. Amusement park rides are disguises for other things. Taken medicinally, periodic trips to the bumper cars can prevent road rage. Cherish the fear in loose bolts, statistical inevitabilities, the substance-abuse problem of the operator as suggested by his glassy stare. The ancient metal seats get repainted every season. Dark metal like a stain where people put their hands. They have yet to invent an amusement park paint that can withstand the corrosive agents in fear-sweat. There is no way to avoid it, all must ride the Cyclone. A loop of ribbon lifted by a breeze, sloping down here, twisting up there. Seems so rickety. Struts and girders, toothpicks and straws. The old scares are the best ones. Couples on dates queue up nervously. The country cousin in from the country is egged on by sadistic kin. They make up scary stories about the fatality rate to scare him but when the restraining bar slams shut are swayed by their own fictions.

TOO LATE to back out. Scream if you think it'll help. Clutch my thigh according to plan. Citizens of this new vertiginous city. Up and down. Reel this way and the ocean is upon you in a wave, in beckoning gloom, reel the other way and slam into highrises, into broad brickfaces. A rollercoaster is your mind trying to reconcile two contradictory propositions. Earth and space, cement and air, city and sea. Life and death. Choose quickly. The city and the sea don't get along, never have. Two trash-talking combatants, two old bitter foes. This ride is them throwing punches and you ride on their arms, dip and rise and coast and roll on shifting muscle and sinew. If only they would stop squabbling over us. Dizzy now. Punchdrunk on the view, tide-tossed and beaten, staggering between what is and what could be. Why doesn't the ref do something. It's a massacre. Close your eyes. Relax—it will all be over before you know it.

BROOKLYN
BRIDGE

⧈

S O S Q U I N T . It's over there, that striated island, cut up carved out and waiting. Pick your favorite cuts and gorge. You can always tell the hungry ones by how they move. Case in point, this one approaching the bridge. Her steps give her away: she has appetites. Her whole history hordes behind her with its unfashionable area code and immigrant spices. The names of her streets commemorate the city's less famous heroes. Mayors and back-room fixers. None of the syllables that built this city, just seeing their names on her mail leaves her famished. Sometimes the wind shifts and ferries aroma across the river. You're hungry, admit it. Grab your forks and knives to get your piece of it.

M U L T I P L E B R I D G E S but this is her favorite. Various anchors hold the island in place so it won't drift away.

You'd try to flee, too, if everyone heaped their dreams upon you. Pack mule and palimpsest. It starts out slowly. At the entrance religious types hawk bean pies and religious literature to cars stalled at the light. Cars wait to enter the borough, she steps on the bridge to exit. Level at first, lulling her. A bridge takes a while to get to the heart of its argument and for a while she is seduced by honey talk, but then she looks to the side. Hardly noticed the gentle lift, but then she looks to the side and she's waist level to buildings. Up in the air before she knew it. Admire the bridge for its exemplary rhetoric, necessary for this rather spectacular leap of faith.

FREE PASSAGE. The only toll is what you need to be rid of. Deposit it in conveniently placed receptacles. Respect the honor system. Refugees pass her going the other way and she wonders what they know that she doesn't. Forsaking what she seeks. Concrete walkway becomes wooden slats and less assured. Going back in time. Farther on it becomes a rope bridge probably, how else to explain their swaying. American flags scarecrow atop the arches. What we'd give for an energetic ripple now and then, it would stir our souls. Nary a breeze this moment. Then she's over water. After land, after industrial waterfront, peek through slats to see the river. Time it right and your spit will hit a tourist on the boat.

LET'S PAUSE a sec to be cowed by this magnificent skyline. So many arrogant edifices, it's like walking into a jerk festival. Maybe you recognize it from posters and television. Looks like a movie set, a false front of industry. Behind those gleaming façades, plywood and paint cans. Against it we are all extras. Walkers add incremental wear and tear to footwear. Joggers speed past walkers, seeing nothing but their inner skylines, long indifferent to the miracles around them. Bicyclists speed past them all, spinning spokes, a different species. He makes up lyrics to his song, humming and snapping his fingers. People who whistle in public get rebuked by glances. Parents shield children with their bodies to protect them from passing crazies. Under her headphones her favorite music is ironic commentary on the spectacle around her. The chorus especially denouncing this panorama with witless enthusiasm. A different atmosphere up here, favoring alternate evolutionary paths. The birds do what they will, equipped with wings.

—

HER LAZY PROGRESS along the bridge is tracked for half an hour by a man in an apartment. Each time she stops, he tries to figure out what she is looking at, thinking of. To be with her, her companion across this thing. Unwitting prop in one man's mania. One speck among many specks. At junctions emergency boxes offer aid but there's no way help would arrive in time. Break down in the middle of the desert. Outlaw territory, between places. Need a tuneup, prescribe this walk. Pop a gasket here and you're on your own. Broken police call boxes report to nowhere. Pick up the receiver to reach a precinct that burned down years ago. What is the nature of the emergency. Shrugs travel poorly through fiber optics. And no one to stop you from tracing a beam to the edge and leaping into space and water. No one could stop you. Traffic slows to rubberneck, other walkers cheer or dissuade, but no preventing hands. All will be revealed in those final seconds before you hit, but at that point no chance to act on those revelations or apologize. Keep moving forward. Please move it along. By making this journey making the case for life or weakness of conviction. Up here everything looks hazy.

—

SIT A SPELL to appreciate. According to ancient calculations, municipal commissions decide where to place
the benches. But they have always tried to regulate your
views. As they sit there listlessly gazing, none suspect his
palm cups her ass beneath denim. This program has been
brought to you by the Department of Public Works. Civil
engineering landmark. Available in die-cast metal at assorted trinket outlets. Bronze plaques here and there maintain history. But nothing to commemorate the magic spots
of people. A couple of years ago he stopped in this very
spot, shook his fist at indifferent skyline and declared, You
can't break me. Now he has two kids and a corner office.
The day after their first night together they walked across
the bridge, seeking its blessing. So far so good. One time
you were caught in the rain and huddled against an arch
for safety. Nowhere to run, prey to the elements as usual.
A trick of the wind left you a tiny dry space until it was
okay to move, but before that moment everything came
into focus and you made pledges. Inflate experiences to
metaphorical dimension. Relate a tale of personal signifi-
cance, receive nondescript nods despite emphatic adjectives. Years ago she picked a window and told herself one
day she would live behind that window and watch them
walk on the bridge like she walks now. Tenants replace
each other and curtains. The curtains of the latest occu-

pants are shut against her and her ilk. Closer to the city, doubtless, but how much closer to what she wants.

LAYERS OF flaking paint pinpoint beautification projects. If only they understood that all that paint was added burden, that it groans beneath our good intentions. Next time will bring it all crashing down. The bridge pants, exhausted. Rattles. Rattles. Every vehicle on the motorway sends its vibration through the bridge and into her soul. If it shakes it can fall. Twin motorways bracket the walking path, squeezing. Given their druthers there'd be no people at all, just tonnage rushing to and fro, not these fleshy vehicles and their hapless pacing. The moment each day when the number of cars going into the island matches the number of cars going out of the island. No flashing alarm, no blinking light, but the bridge looks forward to that moment all day and sighs when it happens. She walks across. A scale inside her seeks equilibrium as she walks this larger scale. Too much of one thing, a mood or an idea, will send her tipping. Her enemies look forward to that moment all day and applaud when it happens.

—

IN THE MIDDLE. Nowhere to go but farther on. Caught in the act of changing your mask, this act of transformation. Don't look back, you will be shocked by negligible progress. A man pitched a tent here once and was hauled away. He told the police, I renounce all boroughs. You have the right to remain. You have the right to shout to the gods. If you have no philosophy one will be appointed to you. Search the eyes of people for kindred glint. Finding no converts despite all your proselytizing. Talking on a cell phone kinda defeats the purpose unless you are describing every detail to the bedridden. Murmur something romantic, will you. It has a certain wavelength. Cables dip and rise, human fate in solid coil. People walk between these tusks, scaling an elephant. Run-of-the-mill fleas. Tourists with cameras speak in the native tongues of the men who built this thing. The bones of their ancestors lie at the bottom among refrigerator doors and license plates. They cannot wave but currents stir their bones and perhaps that is a gesture toward kin. Can't see anything in this murk.

FARTHER ON, the true length of the island is visible. The truth of the matter is not in the window-dressing monstrosities at the foot of the island but the monstrous length of the island behind them. It says, You have not thought this whole thing through. But she's never been one to take a hint. Hardheaded like streets and bridges. None of this means anything to him. What he stands on, what he sees across the river, is no more than the arrogance of men. He is unpopular at parties. Look west for a reminder of oceans, search for proof that you have not always been landlocked. The rest of the world resides in your peripheral vision. A fresh view turns them toward introspection. Introspection is a cheap date up here, wooed by vista and perspective, these cheap flowers. Decide against bad behavior. Decide on better choices. Get rid of him. Get a pet. Little choices magnified to life and death stakes. I can see my house from here.

LOUSY WITH photographers. Why they pick their particular spots is a mystery. They just look and stop and declare, I want this forever. There's something cumulous going on up there and it ruins the light. Minting postcards by the minute. Stand and pose. Click and shudder. Preserving more than sunsets. From now on this place will remind him of their last vacation together whenever he looks at the photographs. Grandchildren look at the photographs later and are unable to marry those images to the drooling elders they know and fear. Mail the photographs you take this day to a friend to maintain the illusion you are still friends. The background says it all: against that skyline we are as brief as a camera flash. Blinded for seconds. But then it returns. That jaw at the foot of the island and its hungry teeth.

THIS SPANS WATER. She spans days. Both fight gravity. This little rivet here is doing all it can but it's only a matter of time. Like you, exerting miraculous will to keep from flying apart. Do not tire. Do not falter. Listen up because I'm only going to say this once: We need all our monuments, no matter what size, carved stone or mortal clay. Do not doubt you inspire with every breath, that every breath is a marvel of engineering. Deserve everything. If not for a plaque shortage she'd have a plaque riveted to her stomach detailing her pertinent details. Space left blank for the day of completion. Up here there are fresh breezes and gulls, brief creatures. She and the bridge have so much on them, possess a weight that will not be blown away.

WHAT DID YOU hope to achieve by this little adventure. Nothing has changed. Nothing ever changes. Presentiment of doom. Closer you get to the other side, the slower you walk. On the other side there is no more dreaming. Just solid ground. So put it off for as long as possible. Here comes another sign, no portent, this one is bolted metal but a sign nonetheless: the mayor welcoming you to the borough of Manhattan. They paste the name of the new mayor over the name of the old mayor to save our tax dollars. A greeting continuous across administrations, timeless and sure. Because no matter their political bent they understand the romance of bridges and have taken this walk more than once. This is nonpartisan emptiness. Just yards to go. Remembering that disappointed feeling she gets each time she reaches the other side, then feeling that disappointed feeling. Check yourself for damage. Everything is where it should be. No miracle. The key to the city fell out of her pocket somewhere along the way and she's level again. Bereft again. Multiple choices into this labyrinth. Today she picks a new route into it, learning from mistakes. Who knows where she will end up this time. Disappear into a crowd. It's right there in the city charter: we have the right to disappear. The city rushes to hide all trace. It's the law.

RUSH HOUR

E K I N G O U T all day and then quitting time and they hit the streets. It's already dark. Their days are growing short. This time of year makes you feel even grayer than usual. Tacked-up cartoons add a little homey touch. They decide what will have to wait until tomorrow, click off desk lights, become visible over cubicle walls. These days disappointment is modular and interchangeable and snaps together easily. According to diagrams fit three words together: See You Tomorrow. People huddle into elevators and ride down into in-betweenness, into the space between work and home that is a kind of dreaming: it's where they go to make sense of what just happened so they can go a little farther.

E S C A P E F R O M midtown. Make a break for the wall or tunnel under. Elementary geometric forms run amok. Architects lay psyche in steel and concrete. Birth of first-born, bye-bye to mistress, alimony checks—it's all there encoded in columns, the features of façades, windows that will not open. Walk in the shadow of subconscious, toil in the monuments to bitter decline. The skyline graphs the hubris of generations, visible for miles, and inevitably all who see it extract the wrong morals from the stories. Common buildings end too soon. Recognize royalty by height, on sight, and memorize their crowns over time. Some of these buildings arrived by tugboat, towed in from the South Pacific islands where they were carved from black volcanic rock. These dark glaciers. So much beneath surfaces. In buildings comprised of other buildings' discarded thirteenth floors, sinister transactions unfold. Office Space Available. Few buildings around here deserve to be people, but judging by the grim procession of faces, some of these folks are halfway to sheetrock. Steel-boned, mortar-blooded. Granite without end.

ORNITHOLOGISTS recognize these corporate peacocks by their pinstripe plumage. What goes through their heads, this species of bird. That pair have the same tailor and when they run into each other feel a great relief. Patchwork and held together by slender threads. Rely on camouflage to keep you safe. So full of suit and briefcase envy that only a really good shoeshine is going to set him right again. Here comes Mr. Bespoke—all they have come to fear lies in his miraculous stitches. When discovered, he will offer no excuse for wearing women's underpants. They're simply more comfortable. The sound of her heels chipping away at office floors makes lesser mortals tremble, but these sneakers downright kiss her feet on the commute. One more day until Casual Friday, goody goody gumdrops. In suspenders, in wingtips, as if dressing up in the language of flight might make them lose the ground and become something better. The wind tunnel round this building finally alerts him that his fly has been open for hours. Bit of a nip in the air tonight.

SUCH CURIOUS rituals fill their days. Pawns and rooks move according to their rules. Take or be taken. Kill or be killed. Knuckle sandwich for the next person who steps on her foot. Summa cum laude from the Institute of Firm Handshakes. Turbine, meet Chassis. Hammer, meet Anvil. Next, exchange cards. Do you have a card. I have a card. Take my card. Do you like my card. Cards rub against each other in wallets and beget little cards. The secret origin of pocket lint. Stabbed by the pin he forgot to take out of his new shirt. Karma's tiny arsenal. They invited her to join them for drinks but she rainchecked because it's been a long day and some people have moved up a bit on the enemies list. Pencil them in for revenge, how's Monday 2:30 look for you. Messy and teeming. Making plans, making haste, making partner. Move move move. The old man trips and falls and gets trampled and they'd help him to his feet but they're late late late.

IF YOU LIVED here you'd be home by now. Still plenty of time to look back over the last few hours and fixate on what did not go as planned. Spasms twist, spasms wrench and warn, spasms pass in a few minutes if history has taught us anything about this ulcer. At the newsstand to pick up antacid he accidentally drops his change into the rows of candy. After hiding behind secretaries and voice mail all day little interactions bring anxiety. Chalk up her swagger through crosswalk to the daily compliments about her skill-set. These laurels are awful comfy, she just might rest a bit. At lunch today they sat him at a civilian table, that's how fast word has spread. Snakes and ladders. Why not remove his desk, bring in a treadmill, hang a carrot from the ceiling and stop all pretense already. So weary— taking credit for other people's work all day really takes a lot out of you. Failing at everything except his fear of success. Passed over yet again. Archivist of slights. Everyone else's good fortune is food out of your mouth or a hug you never got from someone who should have loved you better. Halfway through lunch she realized glass ceilings allow glimpses up into another person's hell. The guys in the mailroom are out to get him, he just knows it. I want your resignation on my desk in the morning.

PEOPLE WHO worked a little later pour over sidewalks, impending competition for seats on transportation. Wave good-night to the security guard. Electronic card keys monitor comings and goings, identifying employees not by dehumanizing numbers but cruel nicknames. Hello, Bucket Face. Surely the clients will gaze upon our lobby and appreciate that we are not messing around. Won't they. Won't they. Looks like marble but in fact is not. Atriums and human ebb-and-flow erode these looming cliffs. Developers plot demise, plot repeal of zoning laws vis-à-vis mandatory public space. Throw 'em a bone. Do public monies actually go to support the conception execution and installation of that hideous public art. Metal twisted into vaguely human shapes. In this autumn light hard to differentiate abstraction. Certainly their wilted postures suggest exposure to blowtorch, crippling temperatures, a variety of crucible. The elements have stripped their weatherproof coating and now they are defenseless. So we make do. Rust slowly, friends, and leave little bits of you wherever you go.

IMPROBABLE as it may be, the day still has a few indignities left. The day waters down indignity with frustration to make it last longer. Abomination, thy name is Subway. He cannot enter. They flood through turnstiles, hips banging rods, and will not let him enter. He must get home, but it's all he can do to get halfway in before another one charges at him. A fish out of school. Everybody knows how it works except for him. All of them from every floor are crammed into this one subway car: the makers of memos, the routers of memos, the indexers filers and shredders of memos, the always-at-their-desks and the never-around. How do they all fit. Squabbling like pigeons over stale crumbs of seats. Everyone thinks they are more deserving, everyone thinks their day has been harder than everyone else's, and everyone is correct.

INTO THE CATHEDRAL. Of course the Dutch were quite shocked to find Grand Central Station under that big pile of dirt. Alas the Indians and their strict no-refund-without-receipt policy. And, lo, as the earth cooled, Grand Central bubbled up through miles of magma, lodged in the crust of this island, settled here. The first immigrant. Still unassimilated. Ever indigestible. The river of skyscrapers flows around it. Travelers swim to it and cling, savoring solid handhold in roaring whitewater. Churches fill up at regular intervals, on a schedule laid out in the business plan. Like the best storms, rush hour starts out as a slight drizzle, then becomes unholy deluge.

CITY NIGHT swallows stars. Painted constellations on the vault of the Main Concourse must suffice. Substitute universe. The Bears and Cancers and Belts up there do not move, shamed into paralysis by the stars shooting across the terminal floor in homebound trajectory. Rack 'em up. The announcer's voice is cue stick cracking these assorted colors into ricochet, into side pockets, into Track 17 Track 18 Track 19. Always a few standing dumbfounded, stupefied by spectacle and speed. If they can just make it to the information booth. Groan and crawl on elbows. On departure boards departing trains scramble up after promotion. He perks up when the name of his town comes over the PA. Save up for a house two stops farther down the line. Drain into exits for trains. Live every minute as if you are late for the last train. Mottoes for sale, get your mottoes here. They meet here every day at this time to hold hands and whisper. Every once in a while for a second against all odds everyone is looking at some kind of clock. Did you remember to save enough energy for one last sprint. What is that dreadful sound like hell's door scraping open and shut: someone in corduroy walks behind them. Destiny approaches in many different ways.

TICKETS, EVERYONE. Hey, Conductor, can you say a little prayer, something pilgrim-oriented. They settle into pews. As luck would have it the kind of person who says, He's a good person to know, sits next to the kind of person who says, I'll set something up. What do they hide in their satchels and bags that they guard so carefully. Voodoo dolls lounge atop last week's earnings reports. Dread the ride home because this might be the day your children discovered the true face of the world and how to explain that to them. What are skinned knees compared to what is in store. What waits for them across thresholds: marriages, mattresses, mortgages of all kinds. The commute is just enough time to get into character and remember lines. That awkward moment this afternoon when she forgot her daughter's name. You have paid to sit, so pray. As if these daily humiliations and sacrifices mean something, are tallied by the ones who keep the books. Tomorrow we pick up where we left off. Sleep tight. Sleep deep. Sleep the sleep of the successful because somehow you made it through the day without anyone finding out that you are a complete fraud.

DOWNTOWN

J U M P I N G R O P E , punching the air and shad-
owboxing especially. The prizefighters warm up for the
big bout. So much on the line. The mirror in the corner
counsels, Keep your fists up and your head down. Then the
bell rings and it's out of apartments, out of workplace per-
sonas, into streets, into nighttime guises. Twilight is a mask
factory.

H A P P Y H O U R descends, this low fog. It's ladies'
night or discounted jello shots or two for one. The bar-
tender supervises distribution of watered-down stash,
picks up bits of conversation. Other people empty her drop
by drop. Solitary drinkers share cautionary tales through
posture. He collects coasters from all over the world. This
one he's got in spades. This is the beer to have when you're
having more than one. Sitting at the bar waiting to be
picked up like in the movies. Or merely saved. Eyes slide

from stool to stool, fingers running across rows of books. Browse this library shelf, linger over spines even as you are browsed in turn, examined, checked out. Certainly there are a few volumes yet unread. Pull the next personality out of your back pocket. Maybe this one will work. He overhears his words coming out of someone else's mouth and wishes his complaints were not so common. Pace yourself. Things are just getting started.

THEY TUMBLE down museum steps after taking in this season's big exhibit. She feels so much more comfortable parroting critics with a bona fide ticket stub in her pocket. When they went into the art house movie it was light out. Reckoning the surcharges on matinees. What do you feel like doing. Dunno. Everybody else knows where the hot new restaurants are. They don't get out as much as they used to. Haunted by the beady little eyes of the babysitter. Depending on what's going on in the rest of the world, for whole minutes he's the worst waiter in the whole world. Protocols for dealing with complainers are taped up by the kitchen door. Think saliva. Seething over appetizers, they save it up for home so they don't fight in the restaurant. It's nice to have an activity or hobby you can share with your spouse. These two have decided on spite and it has brought them closer together. Unlikely as it is, for once they're the well-adjusted couple at the table for four. Eyes roll when he orders off the menu. That looks good. They eat here once a month but something about this meal makes them realize things haven't worked out for a while now and they'll never return. Countdown to symptoms of food poisoning. Would you like dessert. We have a wide assortment of bitters.

THIS MUST BE the place. It's not. This particular street address does not exist. In another city perhaps but not this one or maybe in the future but not now. Then defectors open the door and it begins. He swears he's been here before. Doesn't know a single soul. Lost in the cocktail party. Who to talk to. Anyone. Drain the melted ice again. Go to the bar, hit the bathroom: by the time you return the party will have aligned in your favor. No such luck. Planting this rumor is harder than it first looked. Gardeners advise patience, things take root or don't. Given the choice between two parties that guy over there will always make the wrong decision. Case in point. No prying a certain type from the hors d'oeuvres table. For the last half hour she has been trying to gain converts to grudges but no luck. What does she see in him. He's so transparent. Old enough to be his daughter. For half a minute they inhabit the dream city that lured them from their hometowns but then discover nothing solid beneath their feet and down they go. Quicksand occurs most frequently in movies, then come parties. Mark my words: when they finally teach coffee-table books to walk and talk, the market will fall out of the trophy wife and boy toy business.

HIPSTERS SEEK refuge in church, Our Lady of Perpetual Subculture. There is some discussion as to whether or not they are still cool but then they are calmed by the obscure location and the arrival of their kind. Keep the address to yourself, let the rabble find it for themselves. Wow, this crappy performance art is really making me feel not so terrible about my various emotional issues. He has to duck out early to get back to his bad art. Three cheers for your rich interior life, may it serve you well come rent day. Beer before liquor never sicker. This one's on me. Somehow he ends up buying every round. Hour by hour the customers change, grow humps horns scales. The little noises they make: her boyfriend's out of town, his college roommate is in town, my friend's band is playing downtown. He made too many plans with too many people and things will not turn out okay. She's a little worried because at midnight the new legislation goes into effect and the draconian Save the Drama for Your Mama laws are really going to cramp her style. Hit the town. It hits back.

THE NEWSPAPER write-up contains bad directions to the hot new spot. Suddenly they're on empty streets in unreckoned neighborhoods and must go deeper into darkness before safety. Corners and alleys out of metropolitan fable, bricked-up doorways, newspapers stuntdoubling for tumbleweeds. Streetlights gallow. Footsteps of roving thugs. They ask, Can you hear me. They ask, Is that you beside me or is this the end of it all. Then music enters deep tissues, they see the lights and the mob, but that was real fear and what if word gets out that they're still capable of fear after all these years. Count on one thing, count on this: night keeps its mouth shut. Nightclub doors are shut. This is Rent-A-Bouncer's most popular model. They never blink. New satanic advances make it possible for them to actually appraise the souls of aspiring clubgoers. Seen a certain way, the velvet rope kinda smiles. A delegation of corpses staggers by on structurally unsound heels.

She read an article where it said formaldehyde is in this season. Simple economics: if they only admit the beautiful people, who will pay the cover charge.

AND THEY SAID his shirt was loud. Pantomime desires. One by one the gang goes off on adventures. On waking next afternoon they'll compare notes. Design flaws of the rich and famous. Knock politely on the bathroom door. People are up to no good in there. It's very suspicious. Watch out: it is the nightly running of the anorexic assistants. They squeeze by easily. Everybody's looking so good, everybody's so well put together, I just want to say, Keep up the good work, troops. The DJ has scrutinized evolution and knows the back door into reptilian brainstem. The beat cries mutiny, recruits limbs and hips, strips this vessel of volition. Apparently this song is very popular. Lewd dances trigger responses. Still the wallflower after all these years. To be able to just dance up to somebody and start doing that, whatever that's called. Akimbo things banish drinks to the floor. Elbows heels hands and heads. Beware the lumbering man-child at ten o'clock—they tend to wave their arms when they dance. She looks down at her hips. Not half bad.

—

IT'S A FULL MOON. Lunar effects are readily ob-
servable in emergency rooms and ATM vestibules. People
need more money. If only they could withdraw common
sense. Friends put friends up to ill-advised behavior. Talking to that woman, putting up dukes, stealing furnishings.
She has been following him for twenty blocks and he
still hasn't noticed. The streets at this hour are low comedy. They chant, Girl Fight, Girl Fight. Why does the
crazy person pick on him, is it that obvious. Recognize
them from high school and flee. Past the jazz joint humid
from solos, past the local bar with the earnest singer-
songwriter. After this gig she'll have enough for a new
rhyming dictionary, top of the line, the one with the word
that rhymes with "orange." Bumping into the shop clerk
after hours in this new context. Worlds collide. There's a
cop. Seemed like a good idea at the time. Now he's going
to have to explain how he got this scar an average of
3.5 times a week for the rest of his life. If the victims
all got together they could trace back their misfortunes
to this cursed payphone. It's the only one for miles in
working condition and everything people say on it turns
out bad. Urgent telegram from the Ministry of Unhappy

Thoughts: Been Thinking Stop No Good Will Come From This Stop. Like the moon, you're only good and visible a few days a month. Exerting influence, pulling up whitecaps. The rest of the time falling away, cut up into parts and nobody knows where you are. It's so cold. Just a few more blocks, dear.

MAINTAIN the illusion tonight will be different, wheel in the extra generators if you have to. Plenty of seats in the predictable cafés, no waiting, what'll you have. The menu never changes. Things are pretty much status quo with the sexual-tension friend. Make a note to ramp up machinations for next week. Boys Night Out collides with Girls Night Out over some confusion as to who has the right of way. Perhaps you recognize him from such bungled seductions as Your Front Stoop and Darkened Hallway at the Christmas Party. She has convinced herself she has no secret plan for this encounter. Waiting for the opening in conversation to reveal the true purpose of this meeting. When it comes to romance, he never met a lesson he didn't learn. No, she's never cheated on him but if you put it that way it almost sounds like a dare. Two drinks past the point of being able to suffer chance encounters with vague acquaintances, relatives, people from work. They will report back. One by one we are becoming unrecognizable.

B U T   W A I T , there's more. Under the big top. In tiny rooms of polite talk, in cattlecar taverns, in cavernous clubs, citizens line up for the same amusements, the rigged games and the broken rides. I like your fez. Still plenty of time to suck up, air grievances, expose character flaws. The most important person in the room possesses a gravitational field and cocktail napkins waft toward him. Aim for the soft underbelly, that's their vulnerable point. Anybody got a mint. She must be sleeping on the job because everybody's acting as if they see her for who she truly is. Folks get by on their favorite props, old jokes, some cleavage, Anecdote 7. Test-run Anecdote 7, twice as efficient as Anecdote 6 and only half as long. They applaud his wit. Not a third of the way to the punchline it's clear the joke is going to bomb. From their reaction that word is no longer used in polite company. Did you know that smiling politely burns up the same amount of calories as speaking your mind. He confesses his love when the room momentarily clears. Everybody returns as she is about to make her response. They used to be married and now divvy up the room like they once divvied up friends. Dare you to cross this line. Some rub wedding rings with thumbs when that creature comes into view. He studies her posture as she talks to that dashing stranger. Something is setting off alarms. Smoke, no doubt. Ten bucks says they go home together. Suddenly realizing that you're talking awfully close. Everybody else seems to have left and what does that mean. Somebody stole your coat.

MORE NIGHTMARISH, please. If you insist. This is exactly the sort of behavior her therapist warned her against. He dresses like his friends so they won't suspect he's unlike them. To preempt rejection she dresses to exaggerate her difference when the true enemy is not the world's disdain but its indifference. He is surely the next item in a dreary procession and cannot be seen for all those previous disappointments. Overexplain your latest career decision. How can he even show his face around town after the latest setbacks. People spare a minute or two relishing other people's setbacks before their own inadequacies distract them again. This is his umpteenth pint but he has a hollow leg or some sort of emptiness in himself and doesn't feel the least bit tipsy. What they take for her air of mystery is merely a side effect of her medication. Something's going on under the table. Gargoyles have clambered down from rooftop aeries to replace his friends but he's not sure if he should do anything because they're quite funny actually and much more supportive than his real friends. It's called a tip.

IMPRESS THEM with your selections, jukebox guru. Press the right buttons and she will be brainwashed into the cult of you. Soapbox the better word, for these pamphlets contain his philosophies. Have your songs come on yet. All over town passive-aggressive jukeboxes delay departures. Every selection pulls them this way and that, sad and out to sea unless they outwit the undertow of minor chords. Tonight the song you always despised strides from the jukebox full-bodied and you hear the lyrics for the first time, understand the lyrics for the first time after all these years. This new you with an older soul. Now it's your favorite. All this time singing the wrong words. Some of them have already decided where this night is going. None of them have commented on her engagement ring so she knocks everybody's drinks over. Accidentally on purpose. He spills his guts, it was the last sip that sent him over the edge but she has her hands full with her own loneliness, she's not about to take on his. Reach inside to muzzle the broken part of you that is now talking.

L A S T   C A L L . This is good-night for anyone with a lick of sense. Anyone with a lick of sense is calling it a night. From here on in there are consequences. One more for the road. He pretends he needs convincing. The binge is going swimmingly, thanks for asking. The adjectives that describe the bathrooms are so scarce as to be an endangered species, protected from poaching by government regulation, so use your imagination. So much for the breakfast date. With every passing hour she scratched off another appointment and now her whole day is free. Rumor has it they're open after hours. Something in the way they say, See you soon, crystallizes that their friendship changed months before and in fact they will not see each other for a long time. It has been arranged: leave separately and meet in ten minutes. No one will notice. Everybody knows. Exchange numbers. The little noises they make: we should hang out sometime, we should get together, we should do a lot of things we'll never do. Drunken ladies are crammed into taxicabs by quick-witted friends, out of reach of predators. He won't wake up. This is the last hand. Bet it all on this. Few of them profess to be actors and yet they are naturals for these curbside improvs, the whole clumsy theater of Which way are you going, Do you want to share a cab. They don't want to go home. Someone is waiting for them. Or no one.

THEY HEAD HOME. Remembering too late that he is insufferable on long cab rides. Now Showing: The Return of the Native. In his cups as he slips into his avenues. Buckle up for safety. Ride with him and sooner or later you will hear him say it: I used to live there. His finger jabs as if to poke a hole into night. I used to live there. On Broadway and Fulton and Riverside and Houston he is goddamned irritating, can't keep his mouth shut. I used to live there. In crowded movie theaters when it turns out the location scout knows where to get the best fifty-cent hotdog. On long walks, while flipping through random books of photography, while flying overhead on jet planes: I used to live there. When they least expect it he will say it, apropos of nothing he will say it, because if he hasn't lived there, he will someday. There are always other apartments waiting for him. There is always more city.

—

HELD FAST by red lights in key spots. At the site of yesterday's accident there are shreds of metal and tiny cubes of glass. Each time the light changes, tires spread it far and wide until it's an invisible layer of sorrow across the city. He used to live there on the corner. Who lives in those apartments now, who is using his old phone numbers. Quick math says there's no way he could afford the apartment he grew up in and now he's an exile in his own city. What's there to say as he passes it and all the others, how to communicate this feeling to friends or people who might care. Immensity of the debt. Poverty of citizens. What is there to say as you pass the humble places that helped you in ways you cannot understand, that were there for you on certain nights when you had neither friends nor cabdrivers, only keys. The light changes. Almost home. None too soon.

AFTER ALL THAT worry and the rough seas, night runs aground. Some of them made it to shore after all. He knows a place where they can grab breakfast. Look at the time. Look at me. Look at them holding hands. They talked all night. While everyone else went mad they found each other. Not made for each other but maybe made out of each other. The same substance, the way the city is one substance, every inch of it from one end to the other. Solid. Immutable. Unbreakable. Everybody out. Last stop. Look at the sky. Toward the east side. There's sunlight in its trademarked colors, sunlight charging broken glass, sunlight over tenements at last, and we're safe.

TIMES
SQUARE

IT'S A SICKNESS, really, with telltale symptoms. They say, I do not recognize this place. They say, I feel dizzy and light-headed. Out of sorts. These are epidemic responses, to this kind of dislocation no one is immune. They agree and lament, try to find the words to give to anyone who will listen: It's not the way it used to be. Of course it's not. It's not even what it was five minutes ago.

S A Y H E L L O to dynamo. Heads tilt up forty-five degrees in the standard greeting. If it weren't pinned down by buildings maybe it'd raise a hand in welcome. Instead all it can do is shine, brighter than heaven and easier to get into, an asphalt hereafter. Is that an angel up there or just a forty-foot soda can. That persistent problem of scale. One block is a continent, a nice chunk of planet. Events unfurl in other parts of the globe and march in single file for ticker-tape inspection. River of the world. So happens she was wondering what time it is in Tokyo and there it is. None can deny that these are the most spectacular cave paintings in the history of cave paintings. Electric bill for starters. World Leader. Excite Your Senses. Try The Best. Some of my best friends are slogans. Slogans hang out with each other after they punch out, blink and pulsate, gossip about their friend whose rags-to-riches tale is now the big hit musical, The Catchphrase That Almost Wasn't. Lines around the block. Everybody is a star.

SIMMER THE IDEA of metropolis until it is reduced to a few blocks, sprinkle in a dash of hype and a tablespoon of woe. Add hubris to taste. Serving size: a lot. Some time ago it stopped needing human hands to make it go, for some time now it has been operating on pure will, but performing maintenance lets them sleep a little easier at night. Old-timers balance on rickety ladders and unscrew the dead ones. Replace, replace. Despise it for calling attention to your irrelevance. Pay witness to varieties of obsolescence. The parts she gets offered nowadays mother the ingenues she used to play. The chorus goes, That's What's-her-name, as she passes in sunglasses. First visit in years and looking around he's reminded of the day he realized his son was a better man than he would ever be. Wait your turn, there's enough bitterness to go around. Divert all the energy rushing into this place to power your sub-conscious. It would probably look like this.

LET THE HONKING commence nanoseconds after the light changes, up and down the ave. Honk all you want, little man, you're not going anywhere. Quite a traffic jam we got going on, all of civilization's wrong turns lead us here, bumper to bumper, without insurance or title. She's been through a lot but makeup hides those little dings and dents. Visitors from war-torn lands stroll into this confusion from hotels and feel right at home. Did they leave the iron on, how trustworthy is the caretaker of their pets or children. Nice place to visit but they wouldn't want to live here. Crushed limes at the bottom of jumbo-sized souvenir cups are shorthand for disappointment. Stock up on T-shirts. Ask directions for the fifth time, see if it does any good. Compass needles spin wildly, act hinky when asked to draw a bead on true north. Those with foreign tongues seek after their English lessons, attempt to conjugate this mess. How do you say, I am lost and helpless. How do you say, I am desperate and alone. No need to translate the lights, lights say the same thing in all languages. Look sky-ward and get swept up by the human current, get deposited blocks away, exactly where you need to be. Gawk at the unlikeness of it all, as if human beings slouched from amino acid pools wearing tuxedos and top hats.

BUILD IT BIGGER, better. Brighter and blinding. Buildings get taller, burying us deeper as they play chicken. Race you to heaven, last one up is a rotten egg, floors full of lawyers. Up there in the corporate headquarters of the entertainment combine, executives decide your dream life. Down here vendors hawk heartburn, but at least they wear gloves per health regulations. A man hands out leaflets and they shun him as if he held a sheaf of virus and not merely advertisements for discount prosthetics. Formerly a pickpocket, now he pushes nosebleed seats to faded Broadway shows. The lightbulb salesman on his first visit reels around in glee and says, Now we know where to send all our colored lights. Everybody selling something. Have I mentioned my special introductory offer. The United States Armed Forces recruiting station has some primo real estate, conveniently located in a commotion that turns everybody into an army of one. Protect your borders. Call upon instincts of self-preservation. Hit the arcade. Experts agree video games improve hand-eye coordination. Juvenile delinquents scrounge up quarters for machines, dig deep in pockets for lies to tell cops and parents. Suburban kids trade the better alibis amongst each other. Learn some tricks of the adult world while you're down here, kids. Learn you haven't alibis to spare.

S H O W F O L K   S C U R R Y and scamper, impossible to distinguish from civilians. Magic of the theater. Where is the book of spells that will transform her latest head shots into glossy fashion spreads, insinuate her name into the captions of paparazzi photos. Last night's miscalculations are this morning's blind items. Smile mysteriously when pressed for information. Long as they spell her name right. Wait to be discovered. Break a leg. Opening night for that couple learning warmth in each other's hands. The reviews will come out in the morning. Closing night for that duo making getaway in separate cabs. Let the casting begin anew. Critics sharpen knives, their latest humiliation a whetstone. Wait for your big break, until then you're understudy for that washed-up has-been who's been using your name and face all these years. Maybe one day you'll get to go onstage.

—

NINETY-EIGHT TIMES she's seen it and each performance illuminates some new corner of her soul. Avert eyes from horrible spectacle. The leading man recites his father's insults in his head while his mouth delivers dialogue with perfected passion. So full of feeling up there onstage. This is the mechanical age. What failure in their upbringing pulls them here night after night, audience to this better bauble world of their exile. On New Year's Eve citizens gather and shiver for one last curtain call before it's on to the next production. Watch the ball drop, counterweight to hope. The entire cast signed the program and congratulations, pass out the cigars: it's a souvenir. Wait for idols by the backstage door. Even a single glance would erase so much. When the revolver clicks empty no one will doubt he is her number-one fan.

UNNATURAL nonetheless inspiring analogies from the natural world. A Black Hole. Visible from space, with a gravitational pull so strong that not even life can escape. Subways try to avoid it but every line and route ends up bending into its quantum miseries. A Great Beating Heart. Congested by those who clot this thoroughfare. A healthier diet would include cutting down on us. Or maybe we are less intrusive, more integral. People are pulled into ventricles, then banished to arteries and avenues, feed other neighborhoods with new red-blooded knowledge. What a rush. A Geological Truth. Where two tectonic plates crash into each other egging on earthquake, Broadway slamming into Seventh in ancient dispute. Seismic and measurable in its predictable arguments. How else to explain the rumbling beneath your feet and this feeling of jeopardy.

O H , T H E L I G H T S . At night you need shades. Epileptics beware. These things sparkle: teeth and marquees, wristwatches and new earrings, the occasional soul. Lost in all these gleaming things, how is this last item to stand out. If only those imbeciles in the double-decker tour bus would stop waving at him, they're fanning his insecurities. Against the light what are we but soft meat, held up to X rays and see-through, all weakness and defect on display. Peepworld. Playpen. Pleasure Palace. The famous degradations still pack them in after all these years. This show will never close. No audition required. These new zoning laws, it's been quite a blow to the Kleenex industry, lemme tell ya. That dude in overalls shoves a mop nonetheless.

Sixteen-millimeter movies made for basement projectors have been digitally formatted for home entertainment centers. She prefers the term Adult Film Actress. All the unlucky orphans have fan clubs and websites. And where are all the pimps of yesterday, our assorted Slims and Big Daddys. Long since muscled out by better, more consolidated hustlers, with their stables of trademarked animals and franchise stores. Publicly traded prostitutes stake out corners, broker soft caress of fifty-fifty cotton-poly. How much for a half and half. Instead of anything-you-want, all-you-can-eat in the booths of the cozy theme restaurant. It's better this way. Johns travel in packs, in family herds, with clipped coupons from travel agents. It's better this way, plus they pay taxes and really where would you put a Cadillac anyway with these new Byzantine parking regulations.

THE MOST HARDENED criminals adopt airs. That's Dr. Sleazebag to you. Everything tamed and safe. It's not the way it used to be, she tells her friends from out of town. Smiling as she leads this expedition. Longer she lives here, the more vulgarities to describe to and lord over those who have been here less long. Bonus points if you can name what was in that storefront three failed restaurants ago: a restaurant. Slim plywood stands sentry where buildings used to be, shepherds abyss. Post No Bills. They Post Bills. Check out rubble, cheer cranes hoisting girders. One day he'll see a wrecking ball swing or see the old beast implode in dust or at least hear a loud noise from a couple blocks away and know some lovely destruction is going on nearby. They secretly relish the violence done to their neighborhoods and old haunts because after they're gone they can brag about witness to the heyday. To complain is to belong, possess property. Not rent for once.

K E E P O N the path and you will not see the ruined people, so do not stray from the path. Discount electronics and discount lives. No Money Down. The more accurate signs, the ones advertising Misery and Doom, only get plugged in after midnight. Let's drink in the Old Man Bar. The ancient masters are dead and their secrets were buried with them, so we will never see neon like that again. You are sorely missed. A hush falls across the room when someone says, Liver Transplant. That line of business, you know how it is, feast or famine. He said he wanted to take her photograph, had connections, but only after she makes it down to the street with half of what she went up with will she feel safe. Do not underestimate the will it takes to submit to cliché. Follow the script. It's all make-believe. Like happy endings.

HE DOESN'T remember the exact address but is sure he'll recognize it when he gets there. Old salts list what is bygone. The famous producer has fallen on hard times, the loyal members of his troupe nowhere to be seen because every check he writes these days bounces higher than skyscrapers. No one answers his ad for Beloved Times Square Characters. The sailors on shore leave have shipped out. The cancan girls are on penicillin. The bottom-bill boxers with their punchdrunk epiphanies have retired to condos in Boca, who can blame them really, the mild winters after all. Hair tonic and stogies, peanut shells and bebop, these were the props of the most famous extravaganzas and where do you find them these days. Lament disappearances. Try to light a candle but the match keeps going out. So drafty in these old theaters. As if the old theaters still stand.

SPEAKEASY CITY, major manufacturer of special knocks, codewords, secret ways in. It's been years but be patient. You'll stumble upon it soon. They look in nooks and crannies. The seven-dollar sirloin. Those ribbons she likes. The shop devoted to the sale, upkeep and cultural lore of porkpie hats. Do not be deceived by these new and plastic signs. Need the addresses enough and you will find them. Even landlords earn their wings from time to time. The little store that specializes in Second Acts In American Lives will not budge. It's mostly custom work but the shop doesn't advertise, word of mouth suffices. Right next door is the travel agency that only sells One-Way Tickets Out Of Town. They never have any repeat customers, nonetheless enjoy a steady clientele, a weary stream of the fleeing, the foundering, the failed. These shops have been next door for years and will remain because there is a need. Fix exteriors and repave, spackle down and gussy up, but impossible to hide is true nature. Some things cannot be demolished. Some things reach down and become bedrock. You'll stumble upon it soon because it is important. It's been a while but if he keeps looking he'll find it, the store where he got what he needed that time and look there it is, hasn't changed a bit after all these years and the guy behind the counter remembers his name.

—

THIS CITY is reward for all it will enable you to achieve and punishment for all the crimes it will force you to commit. It's as if she figured out a puzzle as she stood at the corner waiting for the light to change, look at her face, smiling at nothing we can see. At this pure and flickering light. They always feel a bit awkward when they figure out this place. Stalled at the corner, avoided by crowds as if prophets or homeless. Avoid them as you would any angel who brushed against you. The loneliness is the worst, because this knowledge is something that cannot be shared, only suffered. Just as well. Why should anyone else have it easy. Spoken like a true New Yorker.

JFK

✦

IT'S TIME TO GO.

Everything's packed. All the necessary documentation is secure in pockets and pouches. The time passed so quickly. Take a moment to look back and regret all the things you didn't get to do, the places you didn't get to visit. What you did not see. Promise yourself, Maybe next time.

Assuming it will still be here when you finally return.

Sometimes things disappear.

The airport is one of many conveniently located exits. In the beautiful terminals you can get to anywhere in the world. The names of carriers sort them by destination. Shuffle along and do as you're told. Just a matter of time until you are home.

Take your seat.

When you talk about this trip, and you will, because it was quite a journey and you witnessed many things, there were ups and downs, sudden reversals of fortune and last-minute escapes, it was really something, you will see your friends nod in recognition. They will say, That reminds me of, and they will say, I know exactly what you mean. They know what you are talking about before the words are out of your mouth.

Talking about New York is a way of talking about the world.

Wake up. With a shudder finally kicked out of the dream. Impossibly this gigantic creature has taken off. This unlikely gargoyle with impossible wings. How we flutter sometimes. Settle in for the journey and forget. Please forget. Try to forget bit by bit, it will be easier on you. Leave it behind. Then the plane tilts in its escape and over the gray wing the city explodes into view with all its miles and spires and inscrutable hustle and as you try to comprehend this sight you realize that you were never really there at all.

The author would like to thank his friends and neighbors for all their help in getting this thing together: Nicole Aragi, Nicholas Dawidoff, Richard Nash, Tina Pohlman, Bill Thomas, and Kevin Young. These pages would be blank without the love and support of Natasha Stovall.